Sunbeams Through Blankets:

An Inspirational Guide to Surviving Familial Sex Trafficking

Adira James

Copyright 2024 Adira James

Print: 979-8-9853983-6-6
Ebook: 979-8-9853983-7-3

ACKNOWLEDGMENTS

*I dedicate this book to all those
who have endured the unspeakable,*

all those with a warrior's heart,

all those who are healing from trauma,

*and all those who live by the light of
love, learning, and compassion.*

First, I want to thank little me at different ages for enduring and surviving our childhood. I strive to honor my younger voices, and the purity my younger selves protected, by sharing our stories.

To my loving husband, thank you for all of your encouragement and support throughout not only the process of writing this book, but also my continuing journey of healing. I could never have done this without you. Thank you for seeing in me what I could not see in myself, and for reminding me when I waver, that I belong here, that I am loved and loveable, and that you believe in me. I also want to thank my Elders in Ode Remo for their guidance, as well as my Ile.

I have been extremely blessed to have a wonderful support group that I've gained along the way, including Dr. Harriet Mall, Shirlann Krahulec, Dr. Alina Stevenson who I thank expecially for all of your amazing help and expertise, Dr. Michelle Biddinger, and Dr. Sean Conroy. I am beyond appreciative of Marney Keenan for her heartwarming support and her amazing dedication to the search for truth and justice. I thank Melissa Snow for her incredible support, her feedback, the connections she fostered, and her tireless dedication to ending child sex trafficking and empowering survivors. Dr. A. Biddinger was the first doctor I was open with regarding my childhood, and I can't thank him enough for his care, for believing in me, and for listening and being open to learning about my trauma. I also wish to thank the amazing staff at NCMEC; Annabelle Thomson for her belief in me; Elizabeth Wolfe for all her support; Melanie

Williams for all her help and wonderful friendship; the Cherrys, who are always there for a hug when I need it and whose faith in me has given me so much strength; Heather, who encourages me with all her heart; Jermaine Buie for the amazing photographs he took of my artwork; The Refuge and the wonderful people I met there who saved me on so many levels; the new friends that I am making along my healing quest; and the strangers I've received a smile from just when I needed it. To the many others that I haven't named, thank you for believing in me. My gratitude is overflowing.

To the survivors that I have spoken with and met both on Zoom and in person, thank you for opening your hearts to me and listening to mine. We have a bond that is unbreakable, and I wish you only peace, excellent health, and the achievements of your dreams.

Finally, I want to thank The Office, and the positive energy in the Ontario Room where most of my books have been written.

All works of art in this book are original pieces by Adira James.
All photography of the artwork was done by Perfect Light.

Table of Contents

Acknowledgments	i
Author's Note	vii
Preface	ix
Sunbeams Through Blankets	xiii
Baby picture of me	xiv
Blankets	1
Crouching and Sinking	3
Warrior	5
My Recorder	7
Programmed	8
My Best Revenge	9
Trauma and the Brain	10
Seizures	12
Flashback	15
Losing time	18
Watching Flashbacks Like a Movie	21
Separation From Me	22
Dissociation	24
The Woods	26
Letter to My Littles	28
Anchor	31
My Mainstay	33
Untitled	35
How You Met	36
The Show	38
You Can't Make Sense of What Doesn't Make Sense	40
They Trained Me Well for the Race	41
Letter to my parents	43
Untitled	46
The Flash of a Camera	47
Letter to Another's Father	50
Boundaries	53
Rejection is Sometimes Protection	54

Avoidance as a Trauma Response	56
Make Your Own Traditions	58
August	62
Never Mean to Be	65
Grieving	66
Letter to My Baby	68
Eight Little Souls	71
A Mother's Love	73
Be the Person You Needed as a Child	75
Stand Tall	76
The House	78
Letter to the man in the White Coat	80
Survivors	83
Letter to the politicians, judges, and law enforcement officials	85
Grooming	87
Letter to My Nameless Abusers	89
Collage	91
Letter to my Faceless Abusers	93
Hope	95
Coping with Expressions of Trauma	96
Writing	99
The Balloon Story	101
Library is fun	102
What I want to do when I grow up!!!!	103
How to Draw a Pirson	104
Art	105
A Work in Progress	109
Art Therapy Images	110
To Brush and Sweep	117
Splatter	119
Princess	120
Princess	122
Lonely	123
Friends	125
Movies	126
Untitled	127

Containment Bowl	128
Nest Bowl	130
Chocolate	132
Maladaptive Coping Skills	133
Shaken	135
The Floor	137
The Bodega	140
Crumbling	142
Falling	143
Detox	146
Burden	148
My Husband's Eyes	150
Pieces of Me	152
Forgiveness	154
Distract - Pause - Plan	156
Spiritual Growth	158
Growth	160
Integration	161
Through Her Eyes	164
Therapy	165
Using Your Senses	168
More Tips for Grounding	169
Music	171
Land of Silent Notes	172
Calming Exercises for Your Nervous System	174
Breathe In	176
Breathing	178
Present Moment	182
Living a Good Life and Loving Yourself	184
Yoga	185
Meditation	191
Yoga Nidra	193
Self-Care is a Beautiful Thing	200
Water	202
Cooking and Baking	203
Gardening	204
Life Finds a Way	205

Positive Affirmations	206
Affirmations 2	210
Shame	211
Untitled	214
Blinds	215
Bedtime	216
FBI	218
Affirmations 3	222
Truckloads Back to You	223
Rubble	225
Beige	226
Affirmations 1	228
Trauma-Informed Care	229
Safety	231
Letter to School, Law Enforcement, Medical, and Child-Serving Professionals	232
Freedom's Gem	244
My Voice	245
Coping with Trauma by Helping Others	246
Expiration Date	248
Roots and Wings	250
Mountain	251
Hawk	252
Organizations	253
Notes	262
About the Author	266

Author's Note

This guide is a mosaic of my childhood and present-moment truths. In order for the tapestry of my story to carry the reader through a fuller picture of my emotional journey, I did not write this book in a linear fashion. Instead, the prose chapters are interwoven with poetry, drawings and stories from my childhood in addition to poetry, therapeutic artwork, and letters to my perpetrators that I created as an adult.

As you read my book, you will be reading my truth. I have included scenes that best show the nature of the trafficking, and how the effects of my enslavement has imprinted on different parts of myself and my life. I have also included scenes from current situations that show how my trauma manifests today, and I've included a plethora of techniques that I use as I continue on my healing journey.

I have primarily drawn from my memory of being sex trafficked, and the spiral that occurred because of it. In addition to recounting my story through memory, I have used information, stories, and drawings that I discovered in my mother's basement in a box labeled with my name. I have also confirmed specific details by researching county records, and talking with other survivors of the trafficking ring I was sold in.

Due to the sensitive nature of this book, and the open investigation into my case, I have not used any perpetrators' names or professional titles. Although my perpetrators are nameless between these sheets, they have not escaped the truth.

Parts of this guide may be very triggering for the reader because of the subject matter, and the discussion of self-harm and other scenes of physical and mental abuse, but my hope is that my story will help inspire the reader to help create change. The chapters entitled Calming Exercises for Your Nervous System and Breathing include wonderful techniques to help you reconnect to your center if you find your heart or mind racing. Please refer to them anytime you need to, and please reach out to others if parts of my story strike a familiar chord, and you find that you need a little extra support.

I also have also included a chapter entitled Organizations that provides contact information for groups that may be helpful if you need support for yourself or someone you love, if you would like further information on human trafficking, if you need advice on something worrisome that you see in your community, if you want to volunteer for or otherwise support an organization that fights human trafficking or sexual violence, and if you need to report a tip to save a child.

Preface

Survivors of trauma are a strong group of people – in fact, everyone reading this book has survived some sort of trauma in their lives. One of my goals for this book is to inspire ways to multiply the strength that survivors already tap into. So that you, the reader, know what I have gone through in terms of childhood trauma, it's important for you to know how my childhood unfolded.

I was born in Detroit during the late 1970's in a neighborhood called Sherwood Forest. From the outside, it was, and still is, one of the city's most beautiful areas, with mature trees, perfectly manicured lawns, very large brick and stone houses, and shiny Motor City-made cars in the driveways.

After the white flight of the 1960's, the residents of this neighborhood were a racially diverse group of lawyers, doctors, politicians, executives in the thriving auto industry, and other affluent citizens. My mother was Black and Native American, and stayed home after she had her children, while my father was white, and worked in the auto industry as a white-collar worker.

From the outside looking in, my house seemed like the perfect place for a child to grow up, but it was all a facade. I was actually born a slave in a house of nightmares come true. I was a little girl raised in the industry of child sex trafficking. My parents mentally, physically, sexually and emotionally abused me throughout my childhood. in fact, I have no memories from before the abuse began.

Instead of being my saviors and protectors, my parents passed me around to family members (both my mother's and my father's), and sold me to men in a large pedophile ring in the city and suburbs of Detroit from at least age two to twelve. These men were mostly middle-aged white males like my father, many of whom worked at his company. My body bought my father promotions and wealth. It also bought vacations, a nice home, elegant clothing, and local esteem for my parents and our family. I was trafficked out of our home in a coveted neighborhood with a dream-like history. No one would suspect what was happening in my house, my bedroom, my backyard, and in the homes of "clients" I was delivered to, but trafficking doesn't happen only to certain people or in certain places. Unfortunately, it happens everywhere and to anyone.

As you read my story, it is important to understand the definition of child sex trafficking – and more specifically, what familial sex trafficking. According to the National Center for Missing and Exploited Children (NCMEC): "Child sex trafficking is a form of child abuse that occurs when a child under 18 is advertised, solicited or exploited through a commercial sex act. A commercial sex act is any sex act where something of value – such as money, drugs or a place to stay – is given to or received by any person for sexual activity." Familial trafficking is when a "child is trafficked by a relative or person who is perceived by the child to be a family member such as individuals referred to as "auntie" or "uncle" but are not directly related to the child."[1]

This horrific industry is rampant in the United States, and its victims span every category of society. According to the organization's website, NCMEC alone received more than 19,000 reports of possible child sex trafficking in the United States in 2022. These tips included children in all fifty states, Washington DC and Puerto Rico. If that was the number of tips, just imagine how many instances didn't get noticed, reported, or investigated.

Familial sex trafficking is rarely reported. There aren't many statistics to draw from because people don't often report themselves, their significant others, or their family members, and children rarely report their relative(s). Furthermore, children are generally very young when the abuse begins. They are actively kept out of sight and out of reach of the authorities, and because abuse is all the child knows, it is normalized. For instance, I didn't know that my childhood wasn't normal - it was that all I was exposed to from birth. Additionally, if a trafficked child runs away from home, their parents are less likely to report their child missing, or provide authorities with a reason why the child may have left home. Unfortunately, after getting the courage to leave their abusive situations, many runaways end up hooked into the trap of sex trafficking on the streets.

Like so many others, I didn't run away from my abusers as a child, and I didn't tell anyone either – who would I tell? I didn't realize that I had any other option than staying and keeping silent. I was literally programmed to do just that. When my parents and clients threatened me with physical pain and death, and I believed they would follow through with their threats; the evidence was in my punishments. Clients even threatened that if I told, my father would lose his job and my family would be homeless. Because of that, I felt responsible for my family's welfare as early as elementary school. Breaking my silence was not an option. This type of secret can be heavy for anyone, but it can be staggering for a child, and can cause an avalanche of pain. Instead of taking this pain to my grave, or inviting death to me, I am choosing to exhale the truth.

Now I can speak!

I can yell!

And I can help!

With this book, I hope to reach the thousands of sex trafficking victims who have survived, those who have survived other types of trauma, those who care for children or work in child-serving professional positions, and those who serve adult survivors. By sharing what I have gone through and what I have done to try to maneuver through the land mines of healing, I hope to inspire other survivors just as I have been inspired by their strength.

I want to emphasize that healing and surviving don't create a straight trajectory to a pot of perfection at the end of the rainbow. Being a warrior doesn't' mean nothing was taken away from you, it just means you're living and facing your life - past and present - every day. Each day, we have a choice to heal, a choice to make decisions that are in our best interest, and a choice to be free and live in the present moment.

Our growth affects not only us as individuals, but also those around us in positive ways. I truly believe that healing attracts and becomes a catalyst for more healing,

Let's create more positive change and save more lives.

SUNBEAMS THROUGH BLANKETS

How does the sun reach out
of the darkness
with arms
Bright
Full of hope?

It breaks through the void,
The empty
Still
Silence
Of the wooly midnight.

This navy swirls
Weaves
Opaque
Except for the moments broken
By shining stars.

In my childhood bed of trauma
the wooly midnight covered me while I
Laid still,
Holding my breath,
Holding the edges of my blanket.

Waiting.
Waiting for the next round of trauma to begin.

The rays of my childhood heart carefully reached
through the holes of this blanket come daybreak.
Yawning from the effort.

But bold.

BABY PICTURE OF ME

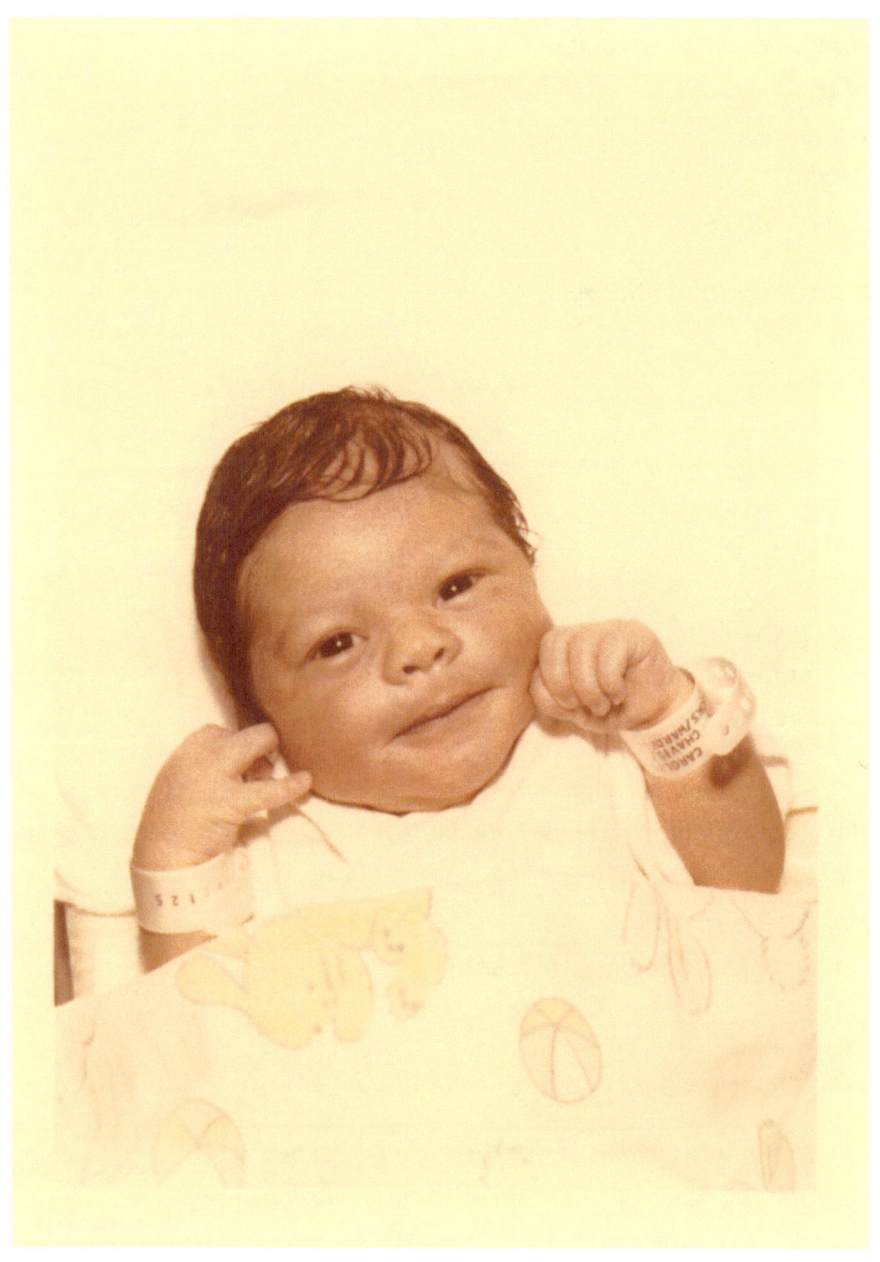

Blankets

The blankets I was swaddled in as a toddler and tucked under my chin as an adolescent were the scariest thing I could see and be enveloped in. They were a haven for evil. Seeing these blankest was scary because I knew what happened beneath and on top of them. My blankets weren't a hiding place from my abuse or a safe haven for sleep. I didn't make them into pretend forts where I could read with a flashlight. Under these blankets, I wasn't a person... I was just something to sell. When my covers reached up and around me, I immediately turned into a doll - a thing - as a client walked into the room. The blankets came to be a symbol of my sexual abuse.

But, because of my perseverance as a child, I survived my abuse and the horrid actions perpetrated on me underneath those covers. Somehow, my heart wasn't calloused from it. My strength shined through the holes in those blankets as a ray of light that nobody could quell. Although they treated me like a thing, my perpetrators didn't succeed in smothering me and turning me into an object.

I've survived and am starting to thrive. My heart is starting to bloom in the present moment; I know this because I'm here right now writing this book. I'm here right now married and living in a beautiful, safe home with pets and a person who I love and who loves me. I have friends who care for me and I care deeply about them. I made it through even though every statistic says I shouldn't have. My heart's light was just too pure, too strong, too determined to be blown out, and thank goodness for the Little mes that saved me so many years ago. Because of them, I am beginning to flourish in the here and now! I draw from their strength and continue to break through the barriers to my success, health, and happiness.

For me, blankets and bed coverings were my symbols of hell, but we all have metaphorical blankets. We all have symbols of trauma that we've shined through. We can catapult ourselves forward through them. Remember, you are a survivor whose light shines through your traumas.

You are a survivor.
You are seen.
You are worthy.
You are a warrior.

CROUCHING AND SINKING

I see you. I really see you and your pain as I look at you crouching – sinking into the rough beige carpet of our living room, just inches from a puzzle I know you weren't allowed to solve. I see your pale skin and your cheeks that are sunken in. I see your baby blue sweatpants and your white long sleeve underwear top with a blue design on it that I can't decipher. I look at you every day, trapped in this photograph with your four-year-old eyes gazing back at me. It's those eyes – my eyes - that capture me. They are set back in puddles of dark circles, but they still shine through the pain.

Your hair is short, fuzzy, and wild. It's just long enough to create a halo of knots that our mother will later struggle to untangled. Struggle until the job is done as you sit silently, unable to cry out with each yank, afraid of what your punishment would be for complaining.

Your mouth is open in speech, but I don't know what you are saying. It's probably an exclamation that you don't want your picture taken. I've always hated having my photo taken because of the abuse we suffered. What I want you to say is "HELP! Help me!" But I know that you can't. You've heard too many threats of extreme punishment or death from mom, dad, and from the many clients in the pedophile ring to tell anyone the truth.

In your open mouth, I can see some of your bottom teeth. Baby teeth that will die in your mouth a few years later, and turn black before dad uses pliers to get them out. "No need for a doctor," he'll say.

As I gaze at you in this picture, I just want to hold you, rock you in my arms, listen to you, and love you. I want to be the hero you needed as you crouched like an animal in need.

That's why I look at you every morning after I've gotten dressed for the day. I want to tell you I love you daily, and I want to be worthy of the sacrifice you endured in order for me to be alive today. I want to remind myself to be your knight in shining armor. I want to remind myself to make good decisions every day to further that goal. And I want you to know that you're *my* hero, all bundled up in that wispy four-year-old frame.

> You're my savior my love! Without *your* courage
> I simply wouldn't be here.

Warrior

Living as a warrior isn't a linear track. Life is fluid, therefore, healing is fluid. There will be times to embrace triumph, and there will be disappointments and failures after which you will find yourself on the ground. What makes you and me warriors isn't the measurement of triumph and defeat, it's the fact that we stand back up and live our lives.

I like to think of the imagery of hiking up a mountain. It may seem like you are stumbling up and down, but you are winding your way upward the entire time. Every time you circle your challenges, you gain more insight and more strength.

Don't think that warriors never feel fear. Acting in spite of your fear is courageous. Being a fighter means that you allow fear to walk with you as you move towards your goals. It may be with you for days, weeks, or years, but you will slowly build more courage, strength, and confidence as you continue on. Before you know it, you will have a greater understanding of yourself and your circumstances, and you'll be free from what weighs you down. Often times, you have to feel fear to feel brave. You can conquer anything.

The heat of opposition can cause the transformation you need. So, when you feel both a sense of becoming in the present moment, while fighting old patterns of unhealthy and unhelpful thoughts, you are in a perfect position to create change within. These moments of change will carry you through to the next positive moment. That is being a warrior.

Honoring and respecting both your wins and your current limitations is your victory. Living your life as a victory while honoring and respecting yourself is imperative. Your current limitations can become triumphs later on, and with time, your wins can be magnified more than you can possibly imagine.

Be kind and compassionate with and to yourself. I know how hard this is, but please don't shame yourself, or harshly criticize yourself when you make mistakes or don't handle a situation the way you would have liked. A recent challenge left me in a puddle on the floor. I had a horrible day, with one negative experience after another. I started to backtrack in my progress, blaming myself and calling myself a loser over and over as each difficult moment passed. Instead of taking time to breathe and slow down the thoughts down in my head, I acted out of fear and chose the reaction that was most comfortable for me: cutting myself in a non-life-threatening spot. I told myself that the only choice for a loser like me was to cut myself or kill myself. I selected the lesser punishment of cutting myself. Immediately after feeling a sense of relief, came a feeling of shame for falling back on my maladaptive bowl of solutions. I felt like anything but a warrior, and I began to beat myself up.

But, as I think of it now, I did choose the lesser of the punishments. I followed through with the option that left me here on earth to make a better choice the next time. I didn't give up. And now I have a better understanding of why cutting isn't the best choice for me anymore on a new whole new level. I've learned that regardless of my intent, one cut can be my demise because I could hit a life-threatening spot by mistake. I wished that I had allowed the negative thoughts to just pass through me as thoughts do, but realizing the possible consequences gives me the power to make that determination the next time I find that I'm harshly punishing myself. With this realization, I have allowed another transformation to take place. I have given myself permission to fall down, make mistakes, and have a setback. I can see these setbacks as opportunities to learn, grow, and expand my healing.

Making a new choice, going to your appointments, sleeping and eating well, continuing to make decisions, and yes, making mistakes, are part of being a warrior. Remember, every breath is an opportunity to make a new determination to honor where you are and how you want your future to be.

> So, please respect yourself and all that you are,
> and live your life with grace.
> Allow yourself to be happy.
> Remember you are amazing!
> You are a warrior!

My Recorder

My body can tell you anything that you want to know.
I've recorded everything that has happened
in my muscles and limbs.
I've stored everything in my heart.

The rope burns still strangle my wrists and ankles.
The many large hands of my abusers
have left fingerprints on my hips and thighs.
The sloppy kisses still surround my lips.
The darkness has kept it all alive.

My body can tell you everything.
I don't need to write it down.

It can speak for itself.
It can speak for me.
It can feel for me.
It can scream for me.

My body is my recorder.
It can tell you everything that you want to know.

Programmed

Being programmed not to tell what was going on at home started earlier than I can remember. I was verbally told that if I talked about the abuse with anyone I would be killed. Those threat were reinforced with acts of cruelty.

I was tied to a radiator or locked in a small dark closet if I dared to disobey my parents or one of the pedophiles in the ring, I was threatened by a client not to tell about the abuse or my family would be left out on the streets homeless. I was even buried up to my neck by one of my clients with my mother standing by after she handed him the shovel. I felt there was no way out, and no way to tell without the consequence of death.

All of the little things – the details of my life - were acts of reinforcement. My closet was divided in half – one side was filled with clothing I could wear to school, and the other had clothing I wore to pedophile parties. There were white tank tops, undershirts, and panties set aside for the clients who came to my room if that was their preference. I even wore different barrettes for clients than I did for school. I had a whole separate identity as a victim of child sex trafficking, and it included uniforms, punishments, and threats.

I spent most of my time at home. As soon as I was out of school for the day, the real reality of my life was in play. School was the acting job that I had to pass in order to survive. As a child, every cell in my body was attuned with the desperation of survival.

My success is that I'm here now learning how to live in the present moment without the programmed narrative taking over. I fight it every day. It was the first program of my life, and it lasted for decades, but I'm still here.

My parents would be horrified to know that I beat it!

My Best Revenge

I was programmed by my parents
and abusers
as a child.

To hate myself in so many ways.

I was taught to
Starve myself as they starved me,
Drink and do drugs as they pumped me full of them,
Self-harm as they injured me,
Try to kill myself as they threatened me with death,
And to feel guilty as they shamed me.

But they couldn't change
what was fundamentally
Me.

No matter what program I was wired to.

They taught me to hate, but I still love and love fully.
They taught me not to trust anyone, yet I trust wholly.
They taught me to live my life tethered to fear,
But I've lived my life guided by courage.
And they taught me to end my life and aspirations,
But I've learned to find happiness.

Happiness.
My best revenge.

Trauma and the Brain

Trauma's effects on the brain are complicated. These effects can touch every part of a person's life, and they can be permanent. According to the research from Boston Clinical Trials, "After any type of trauma (from combat to car accidents, natural disasters to domestic violence, sexual assault to child abuse), the brain and body change. Every cell records memories and every embedded, trauma-related neuropathway has the opportunity to repeatedly reactivate."[2] Sometimes these trauma-related changes can be resolved over time, but with complex trauma that starts during childhood and is repeated over and over, "… the changes evolve into readily apparent symptoms that impair function and present in ways that interfere with jobs, friendships, and relationships."

These changes can express themselves in different parts of the brain, including the overstimulation of the amygdala, which manages threat identification; an underactive hippocampus, which decreases the brain's ability to recognize that memories happened in the past (in other words, memories feel more immediate); and an increase of stress hormones which makes it very difficult for the body to self-regulate. These changes put a survivor on high alert, and can cause the survivor to constantly be in a state of flight or flight.

When I think of all of the potential changes that can happen on a cellular level as a result of complex trauma, it is astounding that I am still functioning. And, it's hard to process the permanence of the things my abusers put on me. It's like their sticky, sweaty hands are still touching my body and reaching into my brain. It's like a horror show.

After all has been said and done, though, I believe it's just another expression of being a warrior. To be able to maneuver through all of the emotional minefields of my day while my brain tricks me into thinking that my abuse is still happening on some level, is the journey of a warrior.

Along the way, I have used therapeutic techniques to help mitigate these effects, such as talk therapy, yoga, art therapy, writing, and breathing. As the book progresses, I will talk you through them.

There are so many warriors out there fighting through these obstacles.

Let's support one another!

Seizures

I have suffered from non-epileptic seizures (NES) for quite some time. NES looks and feels like epileptic seizures. It also takes a period of time for the body to recover from an episode, just like with epileptic seizures. What makes them NES, is that they are caused by mental or emotional triggers, not by a physical issue with the circuitry of the brain like epilepsy. Those who suffer from NES are not aware during their seizures, nor can they consciously control them. NES are also sometimes called pseudoseizures, psychogenic seizures, or dissociative seizures, because the seizure has a psychiatric root and is brought on by extreme psychological duress.[3]

I have a had a few electroencephalograms (EEG) over the last twenty years, confirming that I do not have epilepsy, but the EEG were still abnormal due to excess beta wave activity. The doctor explained that beta waves are rhythms in the brain that are active when you are in a state of waking consciousness, but if they are excessive, they can make you have hyperactive thought patterns. She told me that I had way too many beta waves, and they moved way too quickly. She said that I am essentially living in fight-or-flight mode twenty-four hours a day. I'm on permanent overdrive. I also have overactive or hyperactive reflexes, causing me to twitch and spasm, and briefly lose muscle control at times. This sometimes causes me to fall or drop things.

Because my brain waves are already on high alert, a loud noise, a familiar smell or sound, a familiar situation, or any of my many other triggers can send me into an episode. It may or may not even register in my conscious brain that a sense is triggering me - but my body remembers, and activates the neuropathway to panic. This is so disruptive to my nervous system, that I sometimes have a seizure.

Like most trauma survivors, when I have a flashback or a trigger, it's not that I am noticing that I smell something like the aftershave one of my rapists wore; I actually smell the spicy vanilla scent, and I'm gone.

It's not that I hear a voice that sounds like one of my perpetrators; the person I'm hearing morphs into my attacker, or I go back in time to when I was a victim. My body then follows for the ride.

My seizures do vary. Sometimes, I become physically frozen and am unable to speak. My left side usually begins to curl in on itself. When that happens, I have to ask my husband or someone nearby to uncurl the spasm. At times, I have tremors, and just look like I'm "checking out". Most commonly, my head shakes and my jaw bounces open and closed. I used to have seizures where I was thrown down to the ground and my entire body would convulse. I am thankful that I haven't had a seizure that severe in several years.

I'm not sure why some seizures manifest in different ways. Maybe it has to do with the intensity of the trigger. Unfortunately, most of the time, after the episode, I cannot identify what made me so dangerously overwhelmed that induced the seizure in the first place. I think my lack of ability to pinpoint the catalyst is partially because of the intensity of the trigger, and partially because of the intensity of the seizure. My short-term memory takes a hit every time I have an episode, regardless of the shape it takes.

Unfortunately, there have been several occasions where I have had multiple seizures in a row, leading to physical strokes. I have endured left-side weakness, and lost my speech pattern for weeks - sometimes months - because of these strokes. For me, NES is very debilitating.

When I was newly sober, it was even worse. My brain felt so jumbled. Between not drowning in alcohol and drugs, and drowning in triggers that were no longer masked by the substance abuse, there were times when I couldn't form full sentences. My brain was in an entirely different state, and it was easier for it to get overwhelmed. Since I am determined not to fall into the trap of addiction again, so I am on a journey to figure all of this out the best that I can, and I am trying to be patient with myself during this long healing process.

The medications that prevent epileptic seizures don't work for NES, however, other things have helped: therapy, working through trauma and triggers, attempting to get proper rest so that my brain can heal, and taking medications that help with my anxiety, stabilize my mood, combat depression, and help with flashbacks and night terrors has helped. And invoking self-compassion has been essential. Thankfully, my seizures have started to lessen over the last three months from an average of five per week to an average of two per week, which is amazing for me.

I have started to use more coping mechanisms for seizure recovery, including using my five senses to ground me in the present moment. I also hold ice or running my hands under warm water to fully bring me back after the shaking is over and the confusion has taken a seat in my head. I'm always trying new ways to ground myself to see what works. I am also trying to find a way to shorten the recovery time from hours to an hour and an hour to a half an hour and so forth. I know there isn't a perfect formula for dealing with this form of trauma response, but using the tools in my toolbelt is helping.

Flashback

While walking to the administration offices at one of the rehabilitation centers that I went to, the rain started to spit a bit. It was Florida in May. The sticky summer had already begun, and this particular center was in the Ocala National Forest. The plants surrounding the buildings were beautiful, and the grounds in general created a scene of paradise in the middle of the forest.

As I got closer to the building, I drank in the beautiful wildflowers that lined it. The heat of the pavement I was walking on seemed to sweat in the summer heat. I looked with anticipation at the dark wooden stairs in front of me with anticipation because they would lead me to the relief of air conditioning.

I climbed the stairs to the patio and then it hit me like a ton of bricks. The smell of the rain mixed with the dirt that was trying to drink it up. That smell of rich earth slapped me into a flashback of being buried by one of my clients when I was five years old.

I had accidentally urinated on him while he was raping me, and the burial was my punishment. He dragged me downstairs away from my bedroom – the scene of the crime. He yanked me outside, and made me stand by the garage as he dug a make-shift grave just feet away. My mother had handed him the shovel, and stood across from me with a look I can only describe as satisfaction. I remember his tan, hairy hands clutching the shovel, and his creased cornflower blue polyester pants which ended in brown dress shoes that sank into the grass as he dug into the smoky smelling earth. I don't remember his face, but I remember his strong, gravelly voice. After digging a hole of sufficient size, he instructed me to lie down in it. Then, he began to fill up the hole. With each shovelful of dirt weighing me down, I grew more certain that I was going to die. I was also oddly comforted by the soft and secure feeling of the cool dirt on my back, and the weight of the dirt on top of me – hugging me. It cooled down the tears between my legs, and protected me from him raping me again.

I was both petrified as I drowned, and comforted by the wet dirt that entombed me.

My mother looked down at me in the hole, her cold eyes filled with disdain. When he got to the last shovelful of dirt, he hovered the tool over my face, and a few grains of earth found their way into my mouth. That taste of smokey bitterness. That feeling of granules resting on my front teeth and on my tongue has been seared into my mind and my body's memory. I was coming to terms with my death when he threatened that next time, he would bury me for real. Next time, he would finish the job.

As I scrambled through the flashback in my mind, my body threw itself into a NES on the floor of the patio at the rehab center. Later, I was told that I was shaking and convulsing hard. I don't know how long the seizure lasted, but I came back to the present moment feeling exhausted, laying on the floor of the administration building, with three people surrounding me. A nurse was on the floor with me, and two staff members stood over me with fear in their eyes. They were coaching me back by saying, "You're okay - keep breathing" over and over.

All I could say in response was, "I'm sorry! I'm sorry!" as I tried to find my way fully back to the current reality. In this partially dissociated state, I immediately felt like a burden. Five-year-old me felt like a burden, and how couldn't I? I was told that I would be buried if I misbehaved - that I was going to die. *I* was the problem, not the perpetrator my mother helped, further solidifying that I was in the wrong.

As I lay on the patio floor, the nurse said my blood pressure was extremely high and they needed me to go to the clinic for further evaluation. I was put in a wheelchair because my legs were limp from the seizure and the effects of the flashback. My body just wasn't ready to be back. It was as if it simply wanted to give up, continue laying on the wet earth, and die.

I have that same flashback every time I smell hot, wet earth. Even after all of these years, it still yanks me back. It makes the five-year-old inside of me come out in fear and anxiety. I have to take time to soothe her. I pull out crayons and a coloring book or paper, and I find her favorite stuffed animal, a pink sloth, for her to play with.

Often times, this flashback, along with others, whips me into an NES. Luckily, my NES rarely brings me to my knees anymore. I'm still exhausted afterwards, and need to take a nap. But using my tools to regulate my emotions, I can continue with my day after a couple of hours of recuperation.

LOSING TIME

I'm not asleep.
Not asleep but I'm gone.
For how long?
Maybe 10 min maybe 2 hours,
but I'm adrift for a time.

My body is a shell.

It breathes,
Its heart beats,
Its chest rises and falls in a rhythm
without thought or guidance.

A cavern of breath and boom-ba-boom.
That's all I am.

As a child I was hovering.
Looking down on myself.
Witnessing the torture.
Looking into glazed eyes I barely recognized.

And then I was back suddenly
with as much warning as I left.

Only the sound of my inadvertent squeaks,
hard swallows,
Tears and twitches,
as I settled into present moment.

I noticed the sheets I had yanked and pulled,
And the squeak of the bed

*followed by the grunts, sticky sweat,
and heavy excited breaths
tumbling out of a client's lips.*

I became his candy.
Disappearing a little more with each act of violence.

I had to float to survive.

Booties were replaced
With sneakers,
and then high heels.

Is my body still mine if I'm not in it?
If I leave, is it someone else getting raped?
Beaten?
Restrained?

Now, as I lose time,
I am still completely disconnected from reality.
Experiencing my history from decades ago.

When my eyes come back to now,
sometimes I'm in different clothes.
Sometimes I'm in a different room or closet.
Other times I'm out in the street,
or in my car in a different city.

But I'm here.

I try to make sense of what can never make sense.

But I do know that I'm free now.
I am here now.
I am victorious now.

*The simple fact that I am alive
makes reality my salvation.*

*So I sing a new mantra...
I'm here,
    it's over.
        I'M FREE!*

Watching Flashbacks Like a Movie

I am still trying to master this technique, but being able to watch your flashback go by like a movie is a powerful way to work through a traumatic event. Allowing yourself to step back from all of the senses of the flashback while still processing it in your brain, can help to take the sting out of it.

I first tried using this technique by conjuring up a traumatic scene in my head and watching it happen instead of feeling it happen. I have a recurring flashback from about age ten where I am being chased by a large man. He is a tall white male with gray hair that you can tell used to be blonde. I don't remember the color of his eyes, but in the flashback, I can tell he is furiously coveting me. I don't know how I got the courage to eject myself from the bed and try to run around it, but he chased me, caught me, and slammed me back onto my mattress. It is a petrifying flashback that I have regularly.

In order to feel like I have more command over the scene, I have made myself replay it in a fully conscious state and process it on that plane. By watching the action play out in my head I have gained a little more control. Practicing this way has made it easier to utilize this technique in real time when I do have a flashback. As a result, I have reduced the intensity quite a bit on some of my flashbacks quite a bit.

Whenever you want to introduce a new technique or coping mechanism into your healing routine, please talk with your therapist about it first, but I hope this is something you can try. It may give you significant relief by slowing down and reducing the intensity of a flashback or memory, allowing you to return to your center more quickly.

Separation From Me

How do I dissociate for so long?
I'm so fully empty.
So fully gone from the here and now,
from today's reality of fumbling through paperwork,
and cleaning floors.

My spirit separates from my body,
Where the recordings of my life are laid in stone.

My soul floats, and swims, and runs away
to the forsythia bushes on the edge of the driveway.

Yellow and bright.
A haven from the darkness of life.
A beacon of vitality,
With leaves of voices drawn out for me to hear.
A note that's palpable even.
Yet these voices have long since stopped in actuality.

My heart's essence, with my consciousness
on a road trip to another hemisphere.
Where the sun shines, and peace prevails.

To the prairie of South Dakota
where my family's graves are left.
Some without names, some without flags of
Yellows, reds, blacks, and whites to show the wind blow.

How long was I gone this time?
This trip?

But I'm always back to wake
In the woods.
On my couch.
In my bed.
On the floor.

Dissociation

I can still see myself from the inside of the trunk of a car. I am looking right into my eyes as I lay on my side as if we are twins who were facing each other, our mocha-colored hands almost touching while we sleep soundly. Except we are awake. I can see my twin's foggy dark brown (almost black) eyes. Her short, brown eyelashes are dyed black with mascara. She has thin eyebrows, and dark gray shadows under her eyes, but there is no life behind them. There is no fear, no anger, no tears, and no confusion for six-year-old me. There is just clarity, and emptiness behind those eyes, resignation to what will happen after the trunk opened. She has full pink lips, and a pale forehead, but her flushed cheeks let me know she is alive despite what her eyes say. She is completely dissociated from the here and now except for the will to breathe. My twin knew that after the car stopped for the last time, she would be dragged out of the trunk, taken to the bathroom where ever she was taken, and readied for the client(s) that were waiting.

I am the disconnection. I am able to record in my mind everything that happened to me from that perspective. It is how I developed the photographic memory I am able to access now as a witness, and as a victim.

On this particular day, I was disconnected for the entire transaction, from getting into the trunk, to servicing the clients -two middle-aged white males - and being put back in the trunk. We were in a cabin somewhere up north in Michigan's Upper Peninsula. I remember all of the intense greens in the forest area we were in, and the wooden cabin that looked like it was built in the 1800s. I don't remember what these men smelled like before the abuse, but both of them had a sweet sweaty smell afterwards that resembled the smell of the trunk I was transported in. They wanted me to wear a white and black printed mini dress with black heels for their pleasure, so my mother dressed me in it before I was shipped off. My mother had also done my makeup and straightened and re-curled my kinky hair into bigger waves before we left our house.

One of the clients took me into the cabin, and the other abused me underneath a low green bush. Looking out at my other self, I can see how my form related to theirs, how my body was animated, what abuse my body went through, and details of the client as they related to my position looking on. While dissociated, I retained enough of my essence to be able to follow instructions and act upon them. I was like a marionette doll that had clothing changes depending on the taste of the client.

I bled that day, and I slept on my way home. Both my body and my heart were exhausted. Back home, I crawled out of the trunk back home as one damaged little girl instead of being split in two. As a more complete me, I felt the aftermath of the abuse. I could feel the pain and despair I had to swallow.

Using dissociation as a coping mechanism is such an amazing technology. It got me through so many horrible situations as a child. It was a technique that allowed me to literally and figuratively disconnect from the abuse I had to endure so that I could live another day. It allowed me to stay still, act my part, and go along with the program without fighting back. I learned very early from my father, who was my first rapist, that fighting back meant punishment ranging from harsher sexual abuse and physical and emotional abuse, to being tied in the closet without food. I learned not to use my voice unless it was to act out a script that added to the client's wants and fantasies. I also knew not to cry - crying would distract from the fantasy as well.

Not only was dissociation the only way I could survive, seeing myself and my environment both from outside of myself as well as from behind my eyes has made me a person with an extended level of depth. I am so thankful for it. I have the ability to recall situations from multiple perspectives, and I'm here to talk about it.

Dissociation gives me an opportunity to give myself love from the outside and the inside.

The Woods

Eight parts of me fractured off during childhood's trauma.
Holding hands,
    age 16 at the rear,
        12 with 10,
           7 with 5,
                4 with 3,
                    and 2 with me.

I'm leading them through the forest steadily on foot,
But it seems to swallow us with every step.

We stick together, getting lost in the leaves,
Browns, yellows, greens, surrounding the wood.

Blinding us from the path,
we still pushed on.

Convinced there was shelter for us
    Safe
        Quiet
           Loving
               Nurturing
                   Life.

As we distanced ourselves from danger,
Behind us the fire of abuse, beyond the next hill, our anchor.

The sky the sky, was clear up ahead.
The forest opened its arms ushering us by,

Pulling us towards the clearing, we saw a shed.

Shelter, shelter so excited we could cry.

Tears allowed to fall when we reached the enclosure,
We held onto each other, relief, victory, safe harbor.

LETTER TO MY LITTLES

To all of my Littles,

    I can't thank you enough for shining through all of the abuse we endured. I simply wouldn't be the person that I am without you. I am so sorry that you were forced to fracture off as a two, three, four, five, seven, ten, twelve, and sixteen-year-old in order to allow us to survive. My memory of what was happening to us during each of those years has made it easy for me to understand why you had to fracture off. Again, if you hadn't taken the pain from those incidents with you, I wouldn't be here.

Little two-year-old me had to endure the beginning of the abuse.
Little three-year-old me had to survive a heavy clientele of rapists, and started drinking and taking drugs.
Little four-year-old me had to start to drinking and taking drugs heavily.
Little five-year-old me was buried by a client in our backyard with our mother handing him the shovel.
Little seven-year-old me had tooth after tooth taken out with pliers after they began to rot in our mouth.
Little ten-year-old me had to hide in closets to feel safe and began to cut and starve us.
Little twelve-year-old me had to endure an abortion.
And little sixteen-year-old me tried to kill us over and over as memories haunted us.

    I want you to know that I have made it as an adult, and I am sober and in control now. You don't need to worry anymore about our safety. Even though everything replays in your mind and mine, and the fears and deficits we endured at each age are alive and well, I have my grits together now. You can count on me. I know I haven't always been dependable, but I'm giving you my pledge that you I'm *dependable now..*

I hear your anxiety every time I talk about the trafficking and all of the abuse that went along with that life, but I promise you that it is over, and it's not going to happen again.

I promise you!

I know that the trauma isn't linear and the passage of time isn't linear, but we have been safe for a while – I didn't act like it, so that has made you understandably nervous. My sixteen-year-old part had tried to take control of things, but little twelve-year-old me, you really took on the responsibility of the smaller kids. You are amazing! Your motherly instincts are so spot on, and the rest of the Littles respond to you and believe in you. I pray that you begin to believe in me so I can take the weight off of you. I can take over, and you can be a twelve-year-old. You can mourn the loss of your childhood and I can take on the tears, fears, and anxieties of the smaller kids while supporting you through your pain.

I want to tell you all that I love you!
I want to let you know that you don't need to worry!

When I talk about the abuse in our first book and in this one, I am hoping to create change for the better. I want to inform people about the type of abuse we suffered. I also want to teach them what to look out for so they can help save other children, and empower them to help. I want to empower other survivors as well, and be there to support others who have suffered. I know you want me to help other children. That's what I'm doing by writing this book. The clients and mom and dad can't stop it. They can't manipulate or take control of anything. And they certainly can't hurt us. They have no more power. They don't have a say. They're not a part of our life. We are safe.

So, let me take care of us.
Let me rock you when things are scary.
Let me wipe your tears when the memories start to overwhelm you.

Let me join you in the closet when things feel unsafe, and let me lead you out into the light.

I love you,
   I adore you,
      You are amazing,
      You are powerful,
   You are an inspiration to me and to others.
I am here for you through thick and thin.
      You are the light that allows me to live!

Thank you my loves!

Love,
Me

ANCHOR

I use anchors as a technique to help me take small steps toward healing and growth. I always have different anchors in play from long-term goals and aspirations, to day-to-day goals and needs. For instance, I have a long-term goal of finishing my wall mural, and I have daily goals to do the dishes, clean the litter boxes, and go to bed at a reasonable hour.

The small goals may seem mundane and not things I would need anchors for, but I do. I need to have little grounding goals to measure out my day. I may not be able to finish my wall mural today, but I did the smaller things, so I had some level of success. Having these successes each day helps to boost my self-esteem and they help me keep my focus throughout the day. Each success encapsulates a different level of difficulty for me.

For some, going to bed may not be difficult. When you're tired, you go to bed. But for me, bedtime is a civil war. Part of me is exhausted from the day's activities and fighting to stay in the present moment, and the larger part of me is petrified of my bed, of going to bed, and of going to sleep. Every night, I have to fight hard not to completely dissociate as the sun goes down. It has only been four years since I began consistently going to bed instead of sleeping on the floor. Every night, I thrash in my sleep from night terrors, and I often wake up multiple times a night sweating and often times throwing up. So, you see, it is a really big challenge for me to keep the bedtime anchor on the ocean floor. Me and my trauma yank it up, but I keep trying every night. I keep trying.

My husband is a huge anchor for me. He is a blessing. He is there to listen to me and keep me grounded as best as he can. Unfortunately, I don't always allow him to be there for me, which means he is an anchor that is always there, but sometimes I don't succeed in utilizing his gifts. It's hard to have anchors, but thank goodness I do. I love him I love my cats, and I love my friends. That love alone is an anchor that keeps me alive. That love keeps me here to battle another day, and they make it joyful along the way. Please let the important people in your life be your anchors. It is a rewarding choice!

My coping mechanisms of artwork and journaling are anchors for me as well. Similar to my wall mural, I have journals with daily prompts and daily messages of positivity. These journals are my daily anchors. I also make jewelry and weavings, and I have a goal of making one or the other every day. I have a weekly goal of making new art pieces so that even if I don't complete my daily goal, I have a slightly larger anchor for the weekly goal. Layering your anchors is helpful so that you are not setting yourself up for failure.

I also use longer goals as anchors to help me keep things in perspective and remind me that my future is bright. I put little trips and long excursions on this list. For instance, I am planning a couple of day trips with my husband and a longer trip to Taos, New Mexico in the spring. Planning the trips and having the airline tickets and hotel booked is a nice bit of permanence for my future. What fun anchors, right?

Please try to create anchors in your daily life, weekly life, and monthly life.

They may help you stay down here on earth so that you are here to enjoy what life has to offer.

My Mainstay

If I waver and
allow fears
to overpower me
and my beliefs,

How do I keep moving?

Moving away from all that pulls me
into the darkness.
the nothingness.
Pulling me into a tight embrace.

I look for little breadcrumbs
that end at his heart.

A little trip to plan.
A snuggle with my cats.
An art project.
Writing my thoughts and feelings.

Anything to look forward to
to begin to anchor me here.

But what will keep me here
on earth
in this realm
in this space

is my love.

My mainstay.

My partner in life.

Untitled

The end of this storm is unfortunately
not in sight.

The horizon is a choppy line of the fierce
rising and falling of the dark waves.

The two opposite forces within are struggling
to take hold of my heart,
and cradle my soul.

The desires within are battling to find the
stronger and gentler side of my
heart's work.

The answer is yet untold.

The storm has yet to cease.

And my soul has yet to be cradled
in the loving arms of peace.

                -written when I was 16 years old

How You Met

Before mom died, I found a professional picture that had been taken at your workplace where the two of you met. It was among some paperwork in her basement. The photo itself was trapped in a brown folder, and I didn't know what it was at first. I had tucked it away for years, and happened upon it today. You, mom, are seated in the front row wearing a short, checkered brown dress on with a huge white bow at your neckline, and perfectly white pumps. You, dad, are standing in the back wearing a black suit and tie. It looks just like a school picture with all ten of you in your Sunday best, sweetly posed to perfection. As far as I know, this was the first job for both of you at the company, and it was where you two fell in love swift enough to break up dad's marriage and start on a path of sin together. You look handsome and beautiful to the unknowing eye, but I know what lies behind those eyes. You are far from beautiful. You aren't even decent.

Your path of sin was twofold. The first sin was breaking up of a marriage. The second "sin" was the cultural prejudice you had to bravely take on, and injustice to you and our family. You were a mixed couple, mom being Black and Native American, and dad being white. I remember you telling me that dad's bosses set him aside and advised you not to marry – that miscegenation would wreck his career. This evil concept made you even more courageous for marrying. I wonder with the confidence in your faces in this photo if you had already decided that you were going to break this bigoted concept and follow your hearts. Oh wait - I can barely see a wedding ring on your finger, mom. You had already done it! The simple thin gold band gently shines on your left hand which lies delicately on your lap. A brave statement.

Dad, you would later win a NAACP award for inclusion in the workplace. I wonder if your experience of having a Black wife and having Black children widened your eyes to the concept of inclusion. I can only imagine that it must have. But, how can you be a hero in this sense and such a depraved, sick person in another? How can you accept an award for supporting and championing strangers while selling your child to the wolves day after day? How did you make that work in your head? I know I need to stop asking myself these questions, but I can't seem to stop. I pulled this photo out by mistake, and my emotions of anger and sadness just erupted again. With my emotions come questions that can't possibly be answered.

I don't remember any of the men in the picture by their faces, but I wonder if any of them were my clients. I wonder if this group of co-workers were aware of what type of people you really were.

And how did the two of you start the conversation about abuse? Based on how you look, mom, I don't think you had gotten pregnant yet, and I know you quit working as soon as you had your first child. Did you decide that it would be your second born that you would sell? Or did you make the determination that your little girl – me - in particular would be the victim so that you could rape and abuse me yourself?

I don't know why I bother with my questions. I really don't. I just look at those shining faces, young and full of pride, and the questions just naturally fall out of me. I just know that I deserve answers. I deserve them and little me deserves them. I can't appease either of us.

So, I'll close the photo flap and put it back in the pile I found it in, buried in the mess inside of the Rubbermaid bin of mom's things. Buried for another five years until I pull it out to ask more questions that have no answers.

THE SHOW

My parents put on a show throughout their lives in order to mask the interior darkness that was inside both of them. This show had to outshine the demons they wrestled with from their own childhoods. I know that they weren't trafficked, but I don't think that they could've trafficked me and rendered me helpless without having experiences as a child where they themselves felt helpless. I hold onto that truth, that they were wounded in some way in order to be that evil. I know there are plenty of studies proving that abusers were abused as children. I think that abused children tend to abuse themselves and/or try to help others, or they continue the cycle of abuse with others using the learned behavior of being victimized. I turned my abuse in on myself, but am on a journey to help others.

There were whispers that my father's father abused him and my uncle (who also sexually abused me), and my mother said that one of the temporary tenants in her house growing up gave her money in exchange for molesting her. I think my parents took the stance of *"I was abused, and I survived, so it's okay for me to victimize my child"*. It was an extreme reaction to what they probably went through as children.

Who knows what façades they had to hold up as children in order to survive, but the masks they held as adults involved fancy clothing, fostering a high esteem in the community, and in my mom's case, believing (and telling others) that she believed she was a saint chosen by God to do great things in this world.

They were donors to the opera, the ballet, and the symphony. They were always going to a gala or opening with my mother dressing just shy of couture, and my father always paraded my mother around like a prize because of her outer beauty.

My mother's beauty was a character in itself. She was only happy if she was being noticed for her young smooth skin, her high cheek bones, her perfect figure, and her graceful walk. I'm convinced that she needed lusting looks from men and the women's jealousy to fuel her. She took this attention seeking need to such an extreme, that it became detrimental to me not just psychologically, but it prevented me from getting the right care when I was in need.

Due to the abuse, I was sick quite often, but I was sent to school (if I didn't have a client) anyway. I would inevitably end up in the nurse's office with a fever, throwing up, or with my eyes swollen shut from a punch in the face the day before.

One particular time, I was throwing up, and the nurse called my mom to tell her, "You need to pick her up **now**. She's GREEN!" I think that the nurse was worried about me, and she knew from past experience that my mother would delay picking me up as long as she possibly could. Sometimes she waited so long that I just went home on the bus. When she arrived hours after receiving a call from the nurse, she had on perfect makeup which she called her "war paint". She wore a red leather jacket, a red leather mini skirt, and three-inch heels. She was visibly annoyed that she had to be there, and I got the silent treatment for the rest of the day because not only did she have to come to the school, but she was scolded by the nurse.

My mother's largest and most flamboyant mask was becoming convinced that she was a saint after she started going to bible study. I didn't understand it at first, but I wanted to believe that she was trying to atone for her sins, and would actually do great things in this world like she said she was going to do. I didn't believe she was a saint, but wanted to encourage her to be of service to others. I told her, "I think it would be great if you started to volunteer at different places for different causes, and see what works for you. Something will call to you." She told me, "No, I'll wait for God to tell me." She had no intention of helping others - she just wanted to literally feel holier than though. What a huge mask!

Hiding behind the light of false faith to blind others to her evil ways was deplorable and made me angry. I was angry because of her lies, and angry that I wanted to support her and give her the benefit of the doubt and support her only to be slapped in the face with the reality that she didn't want to be a better person at all.

You Can't Make Sense of What Doesn't Make Sense

At times I have racked my brain with questions surrounding the circumstances of my abuse. I've pulled myself out of the emotion of these queries and really tried to analyze them with the hope of finding answers inside of myself.

"Why did my parents meet?"

"How did they meet, and how did they broach the subject of sexual abuse and their comfort level with it?"

"How did they decide which child to sell?"

I haven't been able to find any answers though, no matter how much time I dedicate myself to contemplation.

I've never asked myself "why me?" because, "why *not* me?" I'm no more special than any other innocent child. That's the only answer I've come up with in all of my time sitting with these thoughts.

So how can I make sense of it? The answer is I can't - you can't make sense of what doesn't make sense. You can't make sense of this type and this magnitude of trauma. There just aren't any answers.

Instead, I've chosen to do with that is to focus on myself and what I *can* do – what *I* can control. I can go to therapy, I can use healthy coping mechanisms when I need them, I can love those around me who deserve of my love, I can work to help others, I can work to make an impact in the fight against child sex trafficking, and I can create hopes and dreams for my future so that I can continue on this path of life.

I can live!

THEY TRAINED ME WELL FOR THE RACE

I took the baton
Passed to me with
Both hands behind my back
Mouth seamed with cotton thread
And cloaked in tape
Silently starving myself to make more room for self-hatred.

One hand was freed.

The second baton grabbed
Pulled the tape off of my lips
Long enough to swallow
Familiar pill after pill.
Forced down
With the warmth of whiskey.

I could pocket the first pass.
The damage was done.

The third baton a knife.
Cutting myself.
My arms,
Thighs,
Stomach,
Wrists red with release with relief.

But my chest rose and fell in rhythm not still.
I was losing.
I lost.

Alive,
My hands returned in prayer behind me.
Shackled with the baton falling down.
My feet separated and chained into place.
I accepted the punishment
And lay flat on the earth.

Nothing to cushion me
From hallucinations
Of men attacking my broken frame
That took turns with men of the flesh.

LETTER TO MY PARENTS

mom and dad,

It's been a couple of years since I last wrote you, and a lot has changed. I have been working on gaining control of my life, and I have gained more inner power. I have twisted my hands away from your cement-like grips.

I'm sure you feel it. There is not much more than mist between us.

I haven't gotten to the point where I am writing your names on dishes and smashing them, or burning your names in a bonfire. I haven't burned the few pictures that I have of you either, but make no mistake, your essence is dissipating from my daily consciousness. The image of you is starting to come to my mind's eye with an almost foggy texture. You're no longer the gleaming twosome that fooled everyone into thinking you were a kind, generous, power couple, instead of the evil incarnate that you were.

Even though I came to the realization long ago that you were both vile, I am not going to think of you as devils anymore, because that gives you too much power. I'm not going to hold hate for you in my heart, because that would mean I am holding you in my heart.

I promise you, there's no room in there for either one of you.

You both took so much from me! You took the child from inside of me. You killed it out of fear for yourselves, and you took away any chance for me to have a child later in life. I was barren at twelve-years-old. You took my childhood away, my innocence away, my sobriety away, and so much more.

After telling you this, I can only imagine that you think you've won – that you've destroyed me – but you didn't. I've won! I'm still here. I'm telling your secrets. I'm empowering myself and other victims and survivors. I'm teaching people how to look for signs of abuse and trafficking. I'm working to try to prevent familial child sex trafficking. I'm still married to the wonderful man that you said would leave me. And I'm growing and learning in spite of you.

YOU DIDN'T WIN!

I still don't understand so much of what you did to me, but evil doesn't make sense does it? I do wonder how you made everything that you did okay within yourselves. Did you ever think of me as your child? Or was I always a commodity – just something you sold – just someone your friends would pay for? Did you decide to spoil ne child, and then sell the second? Was I just something you literally made in order to sell? Was I never real to you?

Was I just something you literally made in order to sell?

I also wonder why you chose not to come clean with me about at least some of your heinous crimes before your deaths. Weren't you afraid of going to hell?

Mom, I asked you questions while you still had your faculties. When I asked you how many men there were that abused me, you said, "More than I can count, it was a long time ago. Get over it." Get over it? And when I was in my late teens and I told you that I remembered the childhood abuse, you said, "You must've liked it - it lasted so long." How could you say those things with a straight face, without at least tears erupting and dirtying your perfect makeup? Even in your eighties, you didn't have the courage to face what you've done. Or maybe you really don't think you did anything wrong – which is even scarier.

I wish you'd apologized for saying those things, and for the actual abuse you inflicted on me. Everything from putting the trainer inside of me every night to stretch me out for clients, to handing that client in the cornflower blue pants a shovel to bury me up to my neck. I wish you had apologized, but I know that was probably too much to expect from a malevolent woman like you.

Dad, I know you were a coward, and I honestly didn't expect you to own up to abusing me, or impregnating me. But the stalking – you could've at least mustered some strength to admit to that. I wish *you'd even taken the next step, and apologized for it. After I attempted to break ties, you swung into my driveway over and over when you saw me at my house. You even tried to time your attacks on me for when I was at my front door so you could grab me and threaten me not to tell anyone about the abuse. I was nineteen-years-old having to deal with you stalking me after I had barely survived you raping me and passing me among your friends in the pedophile ring. You couldn't gather the strength to apologize for any of it? Really?*

Well, mom and dad, I've gained a certain level of peace for myself now. I am going to continue to let you go at the same pace as I am finding myself. I am resisting your control, your faces in my flashbacks, and your abuse in my night terrors. I haven't forgotten anything, and I won't. And don't mistake this letter for me excusing anything you've done, because I'm not. Your behavior was purely despicable, were you. I'm just letting you know that your grip is getting softer, my heart is getting stronger, and you haven't stolen my shine.

I also want to let you know that I've ensured safety for the Littles – the parts inside of me that fractured off from your abuse. You no longer have control over them either. They know that I am in control of us, so they can relax. They know that they don't have to stay hypervigilant and in fear for their live anymore. Be assured that you've lost your grip on them too.

You're both losing me, bit by bit, and I'm going to be happy.
In fact, I AM happy!
Happiness.
That's my best revenge!

-Adira

Untitled

Where were you at night mother?
The eyes were glaring
I was consumed
Burnings
Whipped
Left to wander
Suffer in another's arms
What's that?
Whose there
Another turn

              -Written by me when I was 16 years old

THE FLASH OF A CAMERA

Click.
Slight Pause.
Light.
Zooooom.
And the slight crackle sound of a Polaroid picture being taken of me. I was four years old, and this was one of the many pictures taken of me by my father. I wore a white tank top and nothing else, and he instructed me to take different poses in between the flashes. I remember these photo sessions so vividly that I am desperately trying not to leave my body as I'm writing this.

"Open your legs."
Flash. Crinkle.
And I'm catapulted out of my body.
"Arms open to the side."
Flash. Crackle.
"Touch between your legs."
Flash. Crackle .
And I'm floating above myself.
"Pull up your tank top so daddy can see you better."
Flash. Crinkle.

The worst sessions included pictures taken while I was with a client in the throes of the abuse. More often than not, my dad would take the pictures as I was being raped or molested, but sometimes clients would take their own photos, or my mom would take the pictures of me with a client in the act of the crime. No matter who was on the other side of the black box that flashed at me, it was awful. Even the camera itself, whose tongue would come out to tease me every time a picture spit out, was - and still is - a trigger for me. Then, add the layering of the smell of sweat coming off of many of the men's bodies, the heavy breathing of excitement that crossed their lips, and the clamminess of my skin covering my physical pain, and the memories are even more vivid. Each photo session I remember is a thing of nightmares.

Clients were given these photographs when they left, like they were a prize that they won at the county fair. Knowing that pedophiles historically keep trophies to use for later gratification makes it another form of abuse beyond the initial sexual abuse. They got to take a piece of me with them after they used me. They got a piece of me that they could continually abuse whenever they wanted to. Years later, I'm probably still getting raped over and over.

Because of that extra element of abuse, I believe it is so important to use the verbiage that the National Center for Missing and Exploited Children (NCMEC) uses for these images -child sexual abuse material (CSAM) - instead of the term child pornography. According to NCMEC, "US federal law defines child pornography as any visual depiction of sexually explicit conduct involving a minor (a person less than 18 years old)."[4] The term CSAM reflects what these photographs and videos more accurately are, which is "the sexual abuse and exploitation of children."[5]

When I was about seven, I remember my father buying a video camera, and he began to record movies of me. I wondered even then how much the wad of cash totaled when I saw it being exchanged between the client and my parents. How much was my innocence literally being torn apart worth to them? Was it $20? or $100? Was it a promotion for my father? Or was it front-row theater tickets? I have so many questions that will never be answered.

Over thirty years later, I was so affected by my pain from the CSAM that was taken of me, and my fear that pictures of me might be floating around on the internet, that I opened a case with the FBI. This allowed the agency to send my images to NCMEC to see if I was in their database of unidentified exploited children online. I didn't think that it was likely because the internet didn't exist yet when I was being abused, but I just had to know for sure.

I provided non-exploitive pictures of me from age 2-4 to law enforcement, which they forwarded to NCMEC. NCMEC reviewed its database, but did not have a match for my image to any known pictures online. It was a relief. But only momentarily. I am now in the process of working with law enforcement and NCMEC to share more non-exploitive images from different timeframes during my abuse so the analysts have more to work with when reviewing the database for matches.

I am hoping that no images of me were uploaded to the internet, but I know that doesn't mean that my abusers have stopped using my images for satisfaction in their basements, bedrooms, or attics. I also wonder if any of my abusers' family members have found them in their junk drawer or crawl space, and thrown them out for fear that their loved ones could be revealed as pedophiles. I only hope that someone will have the courage to surrender these images to law enforcement so that I might have the chance to prosecute even one of these men.

I can only hope.

LETTER TO ANOTHER'S FATHER

How dare you! How dare you put me through what you put me through as a child!

You were the one who threatened me with death if I told anyone about you or the rest of the trafficking ring. As you walked me out of the orange two-story brick house you raped me in and proceeded to escort me down the street, you literally pointed to a dog that someone had hung from the trunk of a tree and told me that would be me if I talked.

I was first horrified by the dog hanging from its neck. Not only was it a living being that was killed and on display before my very eyes, but it was a German Shepard which was the dog we had when I was a baby. I had always heard about her and fawned over pictures of her. Shasta was her name. She was beautiful, and all I could see was her hanging from that tree. I pasted my face on the dog's as we walked by the white frame house she hung in front of.

How dare you? How dare you put your daughter in this position where she knows that her father abused a small child - that he paid for a child's body for an hour at a time. How awful it must be for her to know that her father was a trafficker of the innocent just like mine was. I would never want to label someone else's emotions or experiences, but I know at least some of the emotions she must be processing because I have had to internalize and expel similar feelings.

Leave her alone as she processes the level of evil that is inside of you. Leave her alone!

I wonder how close you were with my parents, and how close you were with the rest of the ring. I know you were a photographer. Were you just part of my schedule, or were you the head of photography for the trafficking ring? Or did you have some other title?

I remember you most vividly from the horrifying hanging, but I also know I saw you at various parties as well. Was the orange house yours? Or was it a house that the ring rented for you and others to use?

I know I have so many questions that will never be answered, but I have to get them out. I have to attempt to work through this horror that is laying on my heart.

I was just recently shown a picture of you, and your face is so intimately familiar to me that it makes me sick. I hate your thick eyebrows, your brown eyes, and your smooth skin. I hate everything about you!

When I looked at the picture, I immediately identified you and the Italian horn pendant necklace that mirrored my father's. I remember my father's necklace hitting my face and head as he raped me. Did yours do the same? Did it burn the same hole in my forehead as you abused me? Was the horn part of your partnership? Or was it just a coincidence that both of you liked to have the symbol of the bull around your neck? I looked up the meaning of this pendant, and learned it is supposed to bring good luck to the owner, and protect that person from the evil eye. Did you not know that you were evil yourselves? That pendant was not going to save you.

I wish it would've protected ME from you!

You are evil… or rather you WERE evil. Pure evil. I have to stop thinking of you in the present tense. The time that connected us was decades ago, and you have already died… joining my father in Hell, I'm sure. You've already taken your pound of flesh from me. Leave me alone! Let me sleep! Get out of my head! You're not welcome here. Go back to Hell!

To your daughter, I only wish her peace and healing. My heart goes out to her in a way that you would never be able to understand. My heart goes out to the little girl in her, and to the adult that she is today. Follow her wishes. Whatever she decides. It may be to forgive you, it may be to excommunicate you, or it may be both. Just follow her wishes.

As for me, I will say it again… LEAVE ME ALONE! You are not welcome in my thoughts, my shadow, my days, or my nights.
Goodbye!
Goodbye forever!

-Adira

Boundaries

Boundaries are healthy and appropriate. They are wonderful tools that help me engage with people, and to create space from others. Boundaries aren't mean, unkind, or unhealthy, but I still have a terrible time creating them.

I was never taught boundaries as a child. Well, actually, to be truthful, I was taught only one barrier: not telling anyone about the abuse. But my body was never my own when I was a child and a young adult, so I didn't know that it *could* be my own. I was literally told when to eat and sleep, when to be with clients and which ones, when to sit in a closet, when to wash up, when to urinate in a cup for testing, and so on. I didn't have free will for at least fourteen years, and then I took over the messaging and continued to impose those abusive boundaries on myself after that.

I still have a hard time claiming that space between me and another person or situation as a healthy space that will keep me happier and safer, because I don't even know what that looks like. I have a hard time giving myself the permission to find physical and emotional safety in everyday situations, because I don't think that I deserve it. I've also had a difficult time with the concept that I can ask someone to "please just listen to what I have to say" instead of them telling me what I should do. Additionally, it's hard to say, "now is not a good time for me" instead of absorbing whatever they are doling out. It's so important to be okay with your own needs. It's also a way to reclaim your voice. It is healthy to be heard.

With a lot of therapy, I'm learning that boundaries are a kindness both to me and the other person I'm communicating with. It's okay to make decisions based on my own needs and comfortability, and it's also perfectly fine that it's hard for me to do right now. I'm starting, slowly but surely, to reclaim my voice, to create safety, and to create a healthy bubble around me.

REJECTION IS SOMETIMES PROTECTION

I'm always amazed by the rejection I have experienced because of my abuse. I know that it is a hard thing to think about – someone's parents sex trafficking their own child. But I would never push someone away because of their history. I would never dismiss someone because they're very being is painful and complicated and it's hard to hear about. I feel that we are all complicated in our own way. We all have pain and trauma. My trauma just happens to involve trafficking and severe sexual abuse. I would run towards someone in need of comfort. I don't understand why my family and friends would do the opposite to me.

I have been rejected by my family members, who don't want to believe that my parents could do such a thing because, from the outside, they looked like fine upstanding individuals. I don't know exactly why my family members think I have invented the abuse. Maybe they think I'm mentally ill, maybe they think that I am looking for attention, or maybe they just think I'm a liar. I'm not sure, because they aren't talking to me, which I think is so cowardly. They could at least try to understand me. It's like I'm malignant. They've run from me and my pain like the plague.

Some of my friends - well past friends - have left me as well. One friend grasped onto the fact that I have substance use disorder, and made that a reason for me talking about my abuse. Another friend who I was very close to said to me, "What you're telling me is crazy. So, you've had a mental breakdown, is that it?" I remember it as clearly as the sun, because it cut me so deeply. He disregarded my life and threw away my relevance and my truth like a dirty rag. Once again, instead of talking with me to try to understand that these horrible things happen in the world, and I just happen to be a victim - and survivor - of domestic child sex trafficking, he tossed me aside and ran in the other direction. It's been three and a half years since I decided to share my story with him, and I haven't heard from him since.

Being rejected by friends was somehow worse than being rejected by family because I chose my friends. They were part of my chosen family. They were, or I thought they were, my people.

I was really hurt by this for many months until I spoke with my therapist about it, and she said, "Rejection is sometimes protection", meaning that sometimes it's a blessing to be rejected from a negative situation. She was right! It just clicked in my head that I didn't need the negativity and pain that they were throwing my way. I needed to move on and live my life.

I know my truth, and I no longer have to deal with false accusations and that awful sticky dismissal feeling. I actually feel free now. My small group of friends is amazing, and they support me. I feel loved by them and my husband, and I know what unconditional love feels like.

What a gift!

Avoidance as a Trauma Response

Avoidance is a very common and powerful way for a survivor to handle some of the daily triggers they may suffer from. Avoidance can range from not addressing an emotion or naming it for what it is, to fully dissociating from the situation. I have engaged in every level of avoidance in the past, from losing time by dissociating or drinking my thoughts away, to turning on the television very loud, all so that I don't have to think about myself or my triggers.

There are many things, situations, and sensory reminders that a survivor of trauma may avoid in order to make life less painful. This might mean not going somewhere that looks or feels like the place where a traumatic event happened, not listening to a song or a voice that sounds similar to a situation or a person who perpetrated the trauma, or simply not watching the news where you may potentially see many violent and negative traumatic events. These are all areas where a victim may use avoidance as a coping skill.

Avoidance is a powerful way to cope with trauma and reduce the uneasiness that trauma triggers can bring up, but it isn't always the best way to serve us. In fact, avoidance "can lead to feelings of numbness, where you find it difficult to have both fearful and pleasant or loving feelings."[6] Avoidance not only numbs us to the negative, but it also stops us from processing it. As a result, we don't have the ability to defeat the negativity and move forward. In addition, avoidance can take away the positive because of its numbing attributes. I think that is why I have had such a hard time connecting with the anger I feel about my parents trafficking me. I have emoted about them through letters, one of which you just read, but I just can't bring myself to come face to face with my anger.

Using avoidance can also lead to you to lose out on healthy experiences and opportunities. These healthy experiences may be healing and actually help you expand as a person. Pondering this makes me think of what I've lost and what I've missed out on during periods of my life where avoidance was my template for dealing with trauma.

Recently, I have gone to the opposite extreme of avoidance, and put myself in immersive situations like speaking engagements about my book, writing my books, talking with political figures about familial sex trafficking, and doing book talks and signings. I've done all of these things, and plan to continue doing so, but I still avoid being angry.

I don't want to allow myself to go into a rage - I don't even think I have that in me – and I don't want the trauma that my parent's put me through to change me into a rage-filled person. Sometimes my anger feels like a balloon expanding in my chest. I just want to be able to release a healthy amount of anger so that it doesn't continue to inflate in me. It's a tricky balance that I definitely haven't been able to achieve, but I strive to.

I want to be able to tell my parents' manipulative, angry voices to stop yelling at me to hurt myself. I want to be able to look at their pictures and tell them in a stern voice that they don't have any hold on me. I want to be able to tell their visions in my dreams that they are no longer welcome.

Balancing our emotions, memories, and trauma triggers are all part of being a warrior. Dealing with these things is another example of how the ups and downs of our journeys manifest. Once again, avoidance may not be the best way to deal with our triggers, but it is healthier than a lot of other choices.

>   It may be the best choice for today.

Make Your Own Traditions

Because I essentially have no family, and didn't experience many social traditions when I was a child, I have always struggled with birthdays and holidays.

I've only had one birthday party in my entire life, which was when I was three-years-old. It was a costume party, and I wore a Wonder Woman costume that my mother made. At the start of the party, I felt so special. The red, white and blue outfit was shiny and bright, and it fit me perfectly. I even had a headband and my mother straightened my hair to look like her. I don't remember what shoes I wore, but I'm guessing they were my shiny black saddle shoes that I wore for special occasions.

I can only imagine how cute I was trotting throughout the house clickity-clacking in my shiny shoes pretending to ward off evil with my arm bands. I remember having fun with my friends from preschool for a bit, but it was over when I was asked - and then forced - to play pin the tail on the donkey. I was petrified of wearing a blindfold, which makes sense, since I was bound during some of my abuse, and I was sometimes blindfolded to prevent me from seeing some of the locations where I was sexually abused by clients. At the party, I was berated by my mother for resisting to play. I was humiliated as she insisted that I follow through with the game while calling me names like "baby" and "weakling" in front of the group. She gave me a choice: I could play along, or I would have to leave my own party and would receive a punishment. I don't remember what the punishment was, but it was scary enough that I complied. It didn't matter that I played the game through my tears though, because I was never given another birthday party.

There are many reasons why I've rejected Holiday traditions. On Halloween, I only went trick-or-treating once that I can remember. In Detroit, there were strict curfews, and there was a horrible tradition called Devil's Night the night before Halloween where dozens of buildings were set on fire by criminals. Halloween just wasn't the tradition that it seemed to be in the suburbs. I did dress up at school each year, but in general, I didn't dress up to celebrate the holiday at home.

I did dress up for clients. My memories of dressing up for clients - in fancy gowns, or tight mini-skirts and belly tops, or even my Wonder Woman outfit from my birthday – are much stronger than any positive connotations for Halloween. Additionally, on more than one occasion, my brother would tie me to a chair and make me watch horror films. I remember that one year, he tied me up and made me watch all of the *Friday and 13th* movies. After I was freed, he put on his hockey gear and snuck up on me in the dark. I was petrified! And I was petrified of scary movies from then on.

Christmas also reminds me of the sexual abuse. My father always made a conscious effort to let me know that anything I got for Christmas had been earned by my trafficking. It wasn't an Elf on the Shelf that kept me in line, it was a threat about what would happen if I didn't act well with the clients, didn't follow directions for producing child sexual abuse material (photographs and movies of me naked and in costumes), and didn't comply with his, my brother's, and my mother's sexual abuse. Also, when my dad was drunk (both for Christmas and any other day), I was responsible for taking care of him. He would dress up on Christmas sometimes – for example as an elf - and he would come into my room to assault me while in costume.

I have recently tried to create traditions of my own, which is a much healthier way to experience life! It has been a bit of a struggle to think of different things to do that I feel comfortable with, but it's a journey that has been enjoyable because I'm choosing what I feel works for me. I'm still experimenting, but I've found that these new traditions can be as easy as ordering a type of food and watching a movie. They don't even have to relate to the holiday at hand. I've created a mix of traditions that I am starting to love.

Last year for Halloween, I watched a couple of lightly scary movies with my Husband. This year, I think I will hand out candy to the neighborhood kids. I'm also contemplating getting mums and possibly pumpkins for outside of the house to decorate my yard and bring a little life to the house.

Last Christmas and Hanukkah, I made presents for my friends and husband. I also bought some white twinkle lights that I strung around the workbench in my office, and I bought some small gifts for my husband. I had already showered my friends' children with gifts, and I continued with that tradition. I love seeing their little faces light up, and I channel some of their feeling of joy to my Littles. I have also already planned on baking cookies next year, and sharing them with my friends and their children. I also want to make more of an effort to connect with my chosen family of friends, and possibly take a trip to look at holiday light displays in surrounding neighborhoods.

Last year, I wore green for St Patrick's Day. This probably doesn't seem like a big deal, but for someone who evaded holidays with all of my might, it is a big deal to allow the holiday to enter into my life. And don't worry, I stayed sober.

The only Holiday that I don't think I can participate in the traditions of is Fourth of July because fireworks are such a trigger for me. The noise feels like bombs going off in my head and my heart. My body starts to shake with each of the rocket blasts. I also have a memory of my father lighting off fireworks in our front yard and yelling at me so harshly. I'm not sure if I did anything that deserved punishment or not, but I remember the yelling and him shaking me while grabbing my shoulders. Nothing about Fourth of July seems enchanting to me, at least not yet... but wait. Wait. What does Fourth of July mean, if not freedom? More than anything, I need my truth to be that I'm lovable and that I'm free. I'm an adult who is no longer in the clutches of slavery, so how can I pivot my feelings and claim this holiday? If anything, this is the holiday I need to figure out how to claim the most. So, I have six months from now to figure that out.

As I ponder this, I'm going to remain open to more traditions that I can create or participate in. I think it's a wonderful idea for anyone dealing with trauma memories around the holidays to try to make them your own. When traditions are stripped from you as a child, or even as an adult, you can take them back. You can make decisions to make your life more enjoyable and to inject yourself back into society in a joyous way.

Have fun planning, step by step!

AUGUST

It has taken me forty-six years to realize why August is so difficult for me. I have made so many horrible decisions during this month year after year. Most recently, I had two suicide attempts last year in August. My therapist challenged me to uncover why late July into August are so hard. I had to think about it for about a week until an epiphany came to my mind and lips. That is the exact time that I had my baby ripped from my womb. Of course, there would be a ripple effect from that horrible time in my life.

I remember it so clearly. It was a hot summer day. We didn't have air conditioning, so I was lying in bed sweating with a frozen pack of vegetables melting on my forehead. The blinds in my room were partially closed to keep the full glory of the sun out, while the window was open to allow any wind to grace my skin. I was relaxing after a morning of two clients, and my mother came into my room with a straight forward demeanor. I thought she was going to tell me to get ready for another man, but instead, she handed me a couple of pills, and a short clear glass of watered-down vodka that was mixed with something else I couldn't quite detect. I was still half asleep, or maybe I was dissociated. I blinked my eyes open and propped myself up to drink the mixture she handed me. I looked up midway through, and she looked at me with dead eyes - dead eyes with a little glint of hatred. Her lips moved to say, "Drink this. There's a baby, and this will take care of it."

I wasn't really able to process what she said. Within two seconds, I both found out that I was pregnant and learned that I wouldn't be anymore. I pulled my glass away from my lips only to have her bark, "Drink it all!". I did it. I drank it all. I took what would mark the end of my ability to have children for the rest of my life, but I wasn't able to truly process that in my twelve-year-old brain. How could I? Especially after I was being raped all morning.

I was regularly urinating into Dixie cups for my mother to give to the pediatrician to test. At the time I couldn't conceive of how she knew that I was pregnant. Now I know that he was testing for sexually transmitted diseases, pregnancy, and infections.

I drifted off to sleep from the elixir my mother gave me. I don't know how much time had passed before I woke up with an urgency like I had never felt before. I had to throw up. So, I ran to the bathroom and started to vomit. My head sank farther and farther into the toilet from the effort. Soon after I was done throwing up bile, I started to bleed. I turned around to sit and let the bowl catch what was painfully flowing out of me. I hadn't felt that type of pain before. It was a burning pain. It almost felt like lightning bolts ricocheting in my womb and burning where the bolts landed. I was shaking from head to toe. I can only imagine how pale I was from this horrid experience. I actually passed out at some point, and woke up to my mother slapping me conscious. My heart was racing and roaring, and I saw the mess of blood on the floor where I landed and knew that I was in trouble for it. The hatred in her eyes had grown into embers, and I was waiting for them to spit fire at me.

All she did was instruct me to get up. Then she helped me into bed with a thick pad in my underwear.

I passed out again.

The abortion pills had worked.

The baby was gone.

That level of loss is indescribable. Part of me fractured off to forever be a twelve-year-old after that experience, and the majority of me fell into a deep depression that would never let me go. I even told doctors and friends that my period started when I was thirteen so that I could try to avoid the memories of that fateful day. From then on, I was left to claw myself out of a hole every day to see any light in my life.

No wonder this time of year is so hard. This past late July, I unfortunately fell into a hopeless lane where I felt like a loser, and I ended up cutting myself in a non-life-threatening location. It was after this incident that I finally made the connection. I finally understood that I needed to bring that baby and the twelve-year-old me into my heart and rock them. I need to hold them and love them

and let them know we are all okay every day.
　　Thank goodness we are all okay now.

Never Mean to Be

*I can't stop grieving
for someone that was never meant to be.*

*Someone you created and then
took from me.*

*Wasn't my 12-year-old body
battered enough from the trauma?*

*Of being ravaged over and over,
and passed along a chain gang of felons
to the final stop of pregnancy.*

*You killed it not me.
Was it a he? Or a she?*

*You killed it out of fear
With finality.*

*It was the only chance I was given
To have a baby from then on.*

*I can't stop grieving
For someone that was never meant to be.*

Grieving

Grieving is a necessary part of my life. In order for me to heal from so much that was unfair and painful, I need to allow myself to release it through contemplation and expression. From tears to anger, I need to find ways to process how I'm feeling in a healthy way, and allow my grief process to take place.

My childhood in general was so painful. To be trafficked by the two people who were supposed to be my teachers, my protectors, my cheerleaders, and my saviors is much more than unfair. I wasn't allowed to have a childhood. I started to service clients at age two, so I have no memories from before the abuse. I have no inkling of a healthy relationship with my family. I have no experience of being a healthy child. I grieve for that child – for me. I grieve for the Littles at every age from age two on. I cry for me, and I'm angry for how I was treated. I am sad that I wasn't able to play board games, have other little girls over to my house, and to have birthday parties. I am horrified that my body was never my own, and it was never a safe place to be. I am angry that I have spent decades trying to find a sense of peace that I am still striving for.

I have also had to grieve not having answers of why? who? and for how long? Because my whole childhood was consumed with abuse, I have so many questions about why. I have wondered if my parents had my brother and treated him as the best parents they could be, and decided that their next child would be the one they sold. I have even wondered if they looked at me after I was born and decided at that time that I would make a good profit for them. Letting these questions stay questions is part of my grieving process.

When I asked my mother about a decade before she died, why they decided to abuse me, and she answered with a sharp, "You must have liked it because it lasted so long." It felt like a whipping. I can't possibly express in words how painful that response was. It made me feel like my abuse was my fault, that I must've acted like I liked it, so I was a part of my own abuse, and that I had so many abusers I would forever be waking up to nightmares of another rapist who shines through the clouds of my memories.

I didn't have the courage to ask my mother when the abuse started - if it was before I was two-years-old. I just couldn't do it. I knew I couldn't handle the answer if the abuse did start before then. I was just a baby at the age of two but if it started when I was younger, I would have still been in diapers. The thought is too horrifying to me.

A huge part of my grief is also invested in my first pregnancy... the baby that was forcefully aborted from me at the age of twelve. I was never given the choice to decide if I would keep the baby, or if I would have the baby and put him or her up for adoption. I was never given a choice. I still weep for that child, and the twelve-year-old inside of me does as well. I see her carrying a baby. I have always wondered if that was her baby, or if it was me as a baby. Maybe she cherishes her infant self because she lost her own child. Either way, I grieve along with her.

I also weep for the seven little babies that I conceived in my 20's and 30's. All I wanted, even when I was small child, was to be a mother. These babies weren't able to stay because my womb was a literal landmine due to the scar tissue from my abuse, but they were there for a few hours. They were my babies. They are my babies. I think of them now as forming an egbe (tribe) in the heavens. I believe that all eight babies are together. They know they are related, and they care for each other and support each other in Heaven. I feel like they watch over me as well. They are my angels, and as much as I grieve and cry for them and what I wished would have been, they are with me in my heart always. Even though my arms are empty, my heart is full. I try to hold onto this every day, and on days that are harder, I try to remind myself that these eight souls are forever with me.

Grief is such a powerful process. Without it, I think I would be cemented to my past. As I maneuver through my emotions, I am finding more and more freedom while continuing to honor my past.

LETTER TO MY BABY

HI Baby,

    To be honest, I don't know how I can possibly express the mixture of emotions I feel about you and the abortion that took you away from me. But first of all, I miss you! I only knew that you were in me for a few seconds before they took you away from me, but I miss you. I miss what could've been.

    I know that a piece of me was left in you and a piece of you is still in me. I just hope that the piece of you I carry within me has been able to experience life through my eyes.

    I was robbed of the feeling of you inside of me, kicking, turning and hitting my bladder as you grew in my belly. Now, my womb is empty - scraped with only scar tissue left to hold space. Now, I only have stretch marks from getting heavier instead of from you bulging inside of my tummy.

    Were you a boy or a girl? Would I have dressed you in a blue dress with lacy socks to match? Or a smart looking top with jeans and a cap? Either way, I imagine you with my kinky curly hair and my brown eyes. Either way, you would be my love. I know it won't make sense to a lot of people who may think I was better off without you, but I truly feel your loss as a tragedy.

    Twelve-year-old me is so angry. She is so angry that you were torn out of her. I can hear her weep at night, as she fiercely holds onto the two, three, four, five, seven, and ten-year-old Littles that keep her company. She holds the ghost of you tightly. She has held all of you protectively from me and my addictions, and she has held you to her heart as I tried to kill myself over and over. She has every right to be angry. Not only does she have to deal with adult me making mistake after mistake as I fumble through this thing called living, but she lost you too. Sometimes when I lose time and she is close, I find myself rubbing my tummy in circles. I find myself searching for the feeling of pregnancy that I will never have. Not only was I robbed of you, but I *was robbed of bringing any children into this world.*

You were it for me. You were my baby.

I don't know who your father was. I've always suspected it was my father or my doctor. I let my mind wander when I think about it, and I wonder if I would I have been able to recognize your father when I looked into your eyes. My ancestors said that when a child is born, it looks like the father at first so that there is no mistake about who made you. Would you have had the pointy eyebrows of my father, or the long ears of my pediatrician? Or maybe you would have had the mole on your cheek like one of my biggest clients had.

Most of my clients magically disappeared after the abortion. There was, of course, your grandfather, and a few more, but most of them went away. I had aged out for most of them. I know that you saved me from so many future rapes. It's just so heartbreaking that you had to die in order for that to happen. Thank you for saving me.

I'm so sorry my love.

I'm guessing that if I had been allowed to carry you, I probably would've been sent away until your birth and then you would've been taken from me and put up for adoption. I would've loved to hear your voice, your cry, and your yearning for my arms. I wish I could've felt your fingers curl over mine and seen your hair wriggle around your ears. I wish I was allowed to have memories of you to hold onto.

I had seven very early miscarriages when I tried to have babies with my husband. Seven little souls didn't make it. My womb is a minefield of issues that no baby could survive. Did you try to come through again? If you did, I'm so sorry that you didn't have a soft landing.

After it was obvious that I wasn't going to be your mother, were you born through another family member? Have I met you my sweet?

I also wonder who you would've become. Whoever your father was, he was smart and ambitious. Those are the type of clients I had. And I'm an artist. Would you have been a high-powered executive, or would you have had an art studio where you shared your work with thousands of people? I have dreams for you even though you never stepped a foot on this earth.

I have dreams for you, and I dream about you. You are alive in *me anyway, no matter what happened. You are my baby. I'm crying right now, sniffling and reaching for a tissue as I do every time I think of you, but don't think that it's because I'm sad that you existed. I'm sad because I miss you! So, all I can do is grieve and hope that you are okay.*

I will keep rubbing my tummy, holding you in my heart, and singing you sweet songs. I love you. I always have, and I always will.

Love,
Mommy

Eight Little Souls

That's all I wanted.

To be a Mom.

Ta have a brood of healthy children.

All I wanted was to hold my children close,
rock them to sleep,
kiss them goodnight,
help with their homework,
support them when they win, and if they fail,
and to teach them what good character means.

I wish that my dreams had come true.

I had eight little souls
come and go so quickly from my belly
with a painful finality.

So quickly I couldn't even
get used to the idea that I was a Mom.

And still I weep for them.

I grieve them every day.

Am I still a Mom if someone
tore away the baby in my womb
so forcibly, and without my consent
at the age of 12?

Am I still a Mom of the seven others

I invited inside of me during my 20's
even though they couldn't stay?

I believe that I am.

I am a Mother.

When they arrived,
I made the full commitment from my heart
to raise them and love them,
and I can still hold them close to me there.

Just because my womb was a landmine...
a web of impenetrable scar tissue
from the trauma of the trafficking.

Doesn't mean that I didn't love them
from their beginning to their end here on earth.

I imagine them now in an egbe - a tribe - in the sky.
I believe that they all know each other,
support each other,
and love each other as siblings.

I believe that they are guiding me like angels
as I try to navigate this life.
They are still with me every day.
Reaching out to me for comfort as they comfort me.

I can't wait to see them when my homecoming arrives,
and I can hold them with arms outstretched.

To be a Mom of eight little souls
has been a painful privilege,
but a miracle nonetheless.

A Mother's Love

Walking through Brightmoor,
a neighborhood forgotten.
With burnt houses skirted by open fields,
trees growing out of collapsed windows and folded roofs.
We walked on the path of cracked concrete
to the park ahead.

Squatters have claimed a structure or two,
and artists have claimed even more.
Painted with bright colors and messages of hope
covering the burn,
the fallen,
the disintegrated.

My partner and I passed through, walking hand in hand,
enjoying the renewal.
Life finding a way.
Waving at the few urban farmers
combing through the earth
tending to their flock.

A crack to our right pulled our eyes to an oak.
A kit asleep on a sturdy limb
came tumbling down in a bed of last fall's leaves.
Dust came up to greet her.

We froze.

Waiting for mama raccoon to appear,
to respond to her baby's mew,

her urgent chirp,
which turned quickly to a screech that could rival an owl.

We waited to see if any other ring-tailed babies would appear,
or if their human hands steadily clutched the branch above.
I knelt down to see if any intelligent glowing eyes with painted masks would bob in our direction, or squint against the full sun of the afternoon.

Still still, we heard a rustling.

Agile tiny hands ahead of a plump sow's body
came racing down the trunk to save her kit.
To bring her nursery, her gaze, back to wholeness,
protected among the leaves.

The Lakota say raccoons are mischief-making crafty survivors that teach us how to problem solve,
give to each other, and above all,
to protect each other.

They are right at home here in Brightmoor.
Maybe their energy and wisdom have unknowingly influenced the renewal.
The fight for life by the trees, the animals, and the humans who live there.
Maybe their instruction and their spirit have brought the artists and the farmers to nest.

Pondering this, we walked to the end of the roadway,
smiling at the miracle we witnessed.
That moment of vulnerability and the quick rescue by mama.

The perfect showing of a mother's love.

Be the Person You Needed as a Child

The journey of trying to be the person that I needed as a child has been a journey that has truly changed me for the better. It has made me a better woman. It has also instilled a huge amount of confidence in me, and in the Littles who fractured off from me as a child. It is my supreme goal to cultivate the stability, the compassion, and the strength I needed to have around me as a child. I want to be the hero I longed for.

To me, being a hero for your inner child is simply making decisions every day to live your best self, one moment at a time. And to be clear, being your best self in one moment could mean connecting to your emotions and weeping from a flashback, while in another moment it could mean accomplishing a long-standing goal. It doesn't mean that nothing hurts you, or that nothing was taken away from you by your perpetrator or by a traumatic incident. You can still be the person you needed as a child with scars. You can still be a hero with dips and falls while you sidestep the tragedies in your life.

You're here, you're surviving, and you're at various stages of thriving.

You're a hero.

Stand Tall

The last time that I pulled out this photo, I was giving it to the FBI so that they could turn it over to the National Center for Missing and Exploited Children to search its databases. This image did not come back with a hit, and I've had it tucked away in an envelope ever since – that is until today when I was going through my files.

Looking at this photo of you when we were three years old leaves me with mixed feelings of hurt, anger, and love. Your eyes are dark brown without any discernable sparkle, they are set above dark circles. You still have a bit of chubbiness to your frame that will soon disappear. I can see your little legs popping out from beneath your dress. You have white bobby socks on with red lace-up shoes, and your dress is adorable! It is white with pastel stitching on the top where the rouching is, and a pink gingham lower hem. There looks to be the word "LOVE" spelled out in a gingham fabric that's stitched to the front of the dress with what looks like a little yellow duck and a dinosaur stitched to the top and bottom of the word. You look darling my sweet!

Your arms are full, and each index finger is pointed in a different direction. One hand points in front of you at something out of frame, and the other hand points at your mouth. You have a smile on your adorable face with your tongue poking out to the side and your front teeth showing with a gap between them. The top of your head is cut off, but I can see the ends of your fuzzy pigtails on either side of your head.

You're standing in front of our pool with a yellow lawn chair to your right and a beer can in front of you. I wonder if your hand is pointing at the beer can, not at something completely out of frame like I thought at first. That makes me wonder further if you had a sip of that beer, and you are pointing to your mouth in a gesture that you drank it. We were given alcohol throughout our childhood. I don't remember the first time we were given it, but my first memory of getting drunk was when I was four years old and I was not surprised by the experience. It certainly wouldn't be out of the realm of possibility that we were given alcohol at age three.

I also wonder if that dress was an outfit you were dressed in for the benefit of a client. I remember my mother saying that I was always in pants. I wore my older brother's hand-me-downs, and she said that she felt bad at one point because I was so surprised to see my legs without pants whenever I was in a dress. I already know that there was also a particular client that wanted children that had gaps in their teeth. We were one of his victims because of that.

What if the photo was taken on that bright summer day an hour or so before that client showed up at our house to rape you? What if that smile was the result of alcohol, and would be the last smile of the day? It's so overwhelming to think about that, but it's entirely plausible. In fact, it's probable based on what I know.

So, I'm sorry my sweet. I'm so sorry!

You look beautiful though. You are sweet and beautiful inside and out! Know that you will grow up and survive the abuse you are suffering now, and that we will be okay. Not only will we be okay, but we will work hard to try to save other children. So, stand tall as you are doing in this photograph.

Stand tall.

The House

About eight months ago, I went and took a photograph of the house my pediatrician doctored me in, because I wanted to see if it had changed at all. I only remembered the back of the house, because that was the only entrance I used to come into the house. It still has white siding on the left side of the back of it, and reddish-brown brick on the right side of the back. There is a covering above the back door but it is flat and white instead of the green fabric awning that I distinctly remember billowing and snapping when the wind hit it. There are still iron bars on the back door, which is painted white like the siding.

I wonder how they transformed the inside from the torture chamber I remember, into what I can only assume is a charming house based on the flowers that now line the side and back of the house itself. I remember the door leading directly into an entry way with two or three seats in it. My mom would sit in one of those seats and wait for my session to be over. There was no receptionist, just my doctor to greet us. He was a part of the pedophile ring that passed me around to abuse on all levels. He harmed me just like they rest of them did, but he would do it in his office before or after he gave me my vaccines, applied salves, repaired tears, or gave me medicine to ensure I was sellable again.

He was a middle-aged white male with long features, hair that was turning from gray to white, small eyes behind plastic-looking glasses, curly hairs coming out of his ears, and a larger nose. He was a taller man, and he wore the typical doctor's jacket which he took off when he was ready to repair my injuries, or rape me, revealing a dress shirt and a tie that he would tuck in between the buttons of his shirt presumably so it wouldn't get in the way of his torturous actions.

There was one exam room in this house, and it was where all of the damage was done. It was a sterile, white, square room with one examining table, one sink, a counter with drawers that held suckers and plastic rings that I was allowed to pick from after the abusive session was complete, one set of overhead cabinets, and one white standing scale. Every time I entered the exam room, I would be weighed first, and then I would be undressed by him, or told to undress myself so that he could commence his inspection and rape me. I remember the horrible feeling of the paper under my bottom and back and the sound of it crinkling and crunching under my moving frame. Absolutely horrifying!

    I wonder what that room is used for now. Has it been turned into a breakfast nook? A homework station? Or a storage room? I wish I could find out somehow that it was being used for something pleasant to counter all of the pain that those walls have heard. I wonder if my cries still echo there.

Letter to the Man in the White Coat

To my doctor,

How could you? How could you hurt me the way that you did and still hold the title – the honor – of being a doctor? I looked up the version of the Hippocratic oath that you would most likely have sworn when you became a doctor in 1938, and I was disgusted.

The 1923 Loeb edition of the oath says "Neither will I administer a poison to anybody when asked to do so, nor will I suggest such a course...I will not give to a woman a pessary to cause unwanted abortion...I will abstain from all intentional wrong-doing and harm, especially from abusing the bodies of man, woman, or child..."[7]

You knowingly and willingly went against every part of your oath. You took me into the back of your home and used me like an experiment in your makeshift exam room. You stood there and kissed my mom right before you ushered me into this cold, white, sterile, room where you inspected me for injuries from the sexual abuse. I can still smell your sweet smelling sweat mixed with an aftershave I haven't yet been able to identify as you repaired whatever needed to be repaired on my body. From the tears in my skin, to the burns on my wrists left by ropes that other clients wounded me with, you meticulously washed over my body with your clammy hands and eager eyes. You gave me medication to eliminate any infections, and then you raped me too. No matter what you had to do to make me whole again, you raped me every single time I was in your office. Afterwards, you offered me candy, or fun plastic ring, as a reward for compliance, as if that would or could appease my pain. Unfortunately, when I was a child, I thought that this was what doctors did because you were all I knew from the age of two.

Now I know better, you evil man!

I saw in a calendar labeled "Adira's Baby Book" that I was given the regular immunizations that children receive. The calendar was just the family calendar that was nailed to the wall, but it showed them as appointments, and I trust that you were tasked with administering them. I don't know if you gave me my immunizations on time to make yourself feel better as a doctor, but I think you only did it so that my school had a record of them and didn't question some of the obvious symptoms of abuse and neglect.

Are you wondering how I knew that you became a doctor in 1938? Well, I researched you. I found out when you got married, how many children you had, when you died, and where you went to school. I even found out where you did your medical residency as a doctor. Then, I looked in the Wayne County Register of Deeds and found out that you owned the house you abused me in, and then you transferred the name of the deed to other family members. You transferred it more than once before you sold it right after giving me pills to cause my abortion.

I also looked up the other properties that you owned. You did the same thing with these properties, transferring the deeds to other family members. I haven't gotten the strength to go and look at those properties with my husband, but I definitely plan on doing so. I want to see if I recognize them as one of the locations where I was raped, or where there was a client party. I'm putting all of this information together so I have a clear picture of your life. I plan on gathering up my courage and turning over the information I have compiled on you and the other members of the ring to see if law enforcement will follow through with winding down the rabbit hole of your evil practices. Maybe they can find a link to someone who is still alive. It's scary for me, but not as scary as the way you made me feel as a child. Your secrets are being unfolded, and you will not succeed in tricking me.

I see through your veil.

How many kids did you abuse? How many boys and girls did you repair and then put back on the shelf for the next client to take a part of? Hopefully, there weren't many children who had to endure your true self – a monster in the form of a man. Hopefully, your reach wasn't as far as it seemed when I was a child.

Now back to your final act before you stopped being my doctor. You gave me poison to cause an abortion. I was twelve years old! Twelve! I've always thought that the baby was most likely my father's, because at the time, he was violating me the most. But what did you think? Did you think it was yours? Is that why soon after my mom gave me the pills with a vodka chaser you sold your house and disappeared from my life? Were there any other girls in your "care" that received the same treatment?

I wonder. Was I that scary to you? Was my baby so scary to you that it would warrant closing down your examination room? As I look through all of the records I've found, I think that it can't be a coincidence. Either you were petrified of being found out, or other people in the ring were scared. I guess I should just be happy that I wasn't slotted for a snuff film. If I was, I would've died a pregnant twelve-year-old girl. My legacy would be on a reel of film to torture other little girls and boys into submission.

I can't believe you won awards while you were alive. You also have a memorial in your name at a prestigious hospital. Little does the hospital know that you were pure evil. I wonder how many children you hurt. It sickens me. It literally makes me want to throw up when I think of you. I wonder if I will ever get the courage to tell the hospital what you did so that the memorial can be taken away.

I hope that you got what you deserved after you left this earth. I hope you received a punishment much worse than anything you would have had to endure on earth, and I hope it's for eternity.

I want you to know that I am taking care of myself now.
I am taking care of the little me that you attempted to destroy.
You can't touch me anymore!
You can't hurt me anymore!

GOODBYE!

-Adira

Survivors

I have recently been lucky enough to meet a group of survivors from the pedophile ring that victimized me. We were brought together by a wonderful woman who is fighting to achieve justice for so many of us, both living and deceased.

I will never forget the rainy fall night when we met. I walked into the house and was greeted by our benefactor and another survivor. This survivor was tall and beautiful and gave me a welcoming hug when I walked in. In fact, I think all six of us are beautiful human beings. We all took a risk to be there, and were shining from hope, faith, fear, and relief, all at the same time.

Four of us sat in the living room. My husband, who had come with me for support, was in the next room over. I could feel his hand on my back from the other room, and it gave me so much strength. Three of the survivors were on her television screen connected by Zoom. Just seeing all of us together, connecting in one room, made me tear up.

I had just gotten both of my hips replaced because of congenital issues and the hip dislocations my father forced on me to keep me in place during my abuse. I was raw from emotional and physical pain, but I was sweetly seated in a comfortable chair, and was ready to connect with these amazing survivors. We all brought pictures from our childhoods. I brought a couple of pictures of me, and a couple of pictures of my parents. One of the survivors recognized my father by his picture and blurted out his name. It took my breath away to hear her voice call my father's name with such haunting in her voice. She said, "I know him from so many of the parties." I gulped with guilt knowing that he had most likely abused her or another child at those parties. I asked if anyone else recognized me or my parents. They did not, but they were older than me, so we may not have been at the same locations at the same time.

As we went through other pictures, the same survivor and I both recognized my pediatrician, two politicians, and several other people. I also recognized her father, and blurted out, "I know him! I know his face! I just don't know his name." We looked at each other with compassion and a sense of knowing without saying a word.

The meeting lasted about two hours. By then, we were all spent with emotion. I cried the entire way home, with shock, with relief, and with a need to release. I had been given such a gift of affirmation. Everything that I remembered was corroborated, and all of my fears were valid. I was a part of a tribe of women and men who had survived hell.

But we made it!

I have touched base with the survivor who recognized my father several times since then, and we have connected on even more memories... more horrors.

We are connected forever.

Feeling the strength of the survivors I met with from the ring I was victimized by made me search for other survivors, and I was recently connected to a group of other familial sex trafficking survivors. They are an incredible group of women. The small group consists of people who have shared this specific trauma, and it has been very healing to meet them and talk about our commonalities and needs. I hope to continue meeting with them, and I urge others to reach out to support groups where people will understand what you are going through because of their own lived experiences.

I hope for peace and warmth for all of the survivors out there.

LETTER TO THE POLITICIANS, JUDGES, AND LAW ENFORCEMENT OFFICIALS

Dear men of power,

I haven't written to you yet, because, quite frankly, I've been scared of you. You were all powerful people in the community and you abused that power when you abused children. Some of you were sharks on the road and had seemingly un-ending power with night sticks and badges. Some of you were on the bench of the law, able to level a table with one swift hit from your gavel. Some of you traveled from home to the capital to change laws and seemingly do the public's work for them. All of you made me a piece of property that you could use up and pass to the next, and I hate you for it.

Now, I hate you more than I'm scared of you. Know that just because I'm not using your names, that doesn't mean I'm a petrified five-year-old. I'm an adult. I'm equal to you in the flesh, and I'm in control of my life.

Part of my strength has come from meeting another one of your victims. Yes, that's right! I have met another brave woman who survived you. We met with each other, and we looked at pictures I've taken of houses I remember being abused in, and pored over pictures of men like you that I remember as my clients. She and I named many of the same people ... you! We have corroborated on so much of one another's torture. Along with your faces, we remember many of the same places, from offices, to a theatre in downtown Detroit. We even talked about the place where our "party" dresses came from.

It's probably one of your worst nightmares for two or more of your victims to talk with each other and strengthen each other as we process our collective pain together. Your secrets are out, and not only because of me.

When I was a child, you were larger than life. You were clients that had full control of me. You were men in uniforms of authority whose mouths threatened me not to tell. As an adult, I know you are evil, sick individuals that used your power to petrify a little girl over and over. You are rapists. You're just sadistic rapists that don't deserve to have one bit of happiness in your lives. I will never forget you as the slimy, scary, sinful beings that you are (or were if you've passed on from this earth). I will never forget your hot breath and heavy bodies either, but I will remember the truth of you - not the huge monsters that my child's eyes made you into. You are all middle-aged white males... just men.

I wonder how many lives you devoured in the pedophile ring? How many little girls and/or boys did you petrify with your stature and your abuse? I want to hug all of them. I want to snuggle all of those little girls and boys, including little me, on my lap now. I want to tell them that it's over... it's really over now. I want them to know that they are free from you and you no longer have a hold on any of us.

This is my wish for you - NO MORE CONTROL!

This is my wish for me and the other little girls and boys – FREEDOM!

-Adira

GROOMING

Grooming can take on many different forms, and it can look very different depending on the perpetrator's approach and technique. Pedophiles are very manipulative. Using their very nature, they coerce children into their cars, into their homes, and into their beds, by promising things like treats or toys. Before the child knows it, they are in the pedophile's clutches.

A pedophile neighbor, for example, may talk to the children in the neighborhood about something exciting like a video game that he has inside of his home. Then, he may find out what the parents of a few of the children's schedules are so he knows when a child may be alone. After that, he may say something as easy as, "come over after school. We can play this new game for a while, and I'll have you home before your mom gets home." to the child. Using the familiarity of being a neighbor, and the draw of a new game, could be enough grooming to get a child into his home.

Children aren't the only ones who are tricked, however. Pedophiles can influence adults as well. They wield their sword of manipulation on adults to gain access to the children in their lives. I've previously used an example of an uncle who convinces his sister, who is a single mother, that he is taking her son fishing so that the boy has bonding time with a man. He could tell her that he wants to help this boy because his dad isn't around, and if her son comes home upset, he may say, "Oh, we were just talking about his dad, and he was crying because he's so happy to spend time with me. Just give him some time, and more time with me, and he will be okay." That mother's first instinct would probably be to trust her brother and encourage similar outings because she wants her son to be happy and have a strong male role model. The perpetrator was manipulating her into making a dangerous choice. Remember, pedophiles can be excellent and creative liars to whomever they want to exploit or influence. None of us are immune to their tactics.

It isn't talked about very often, but perpetrators frequently groom children by using adult pornography as a tool to train the child on what to do. My parents used this technique. I remember being shown pornographic films and being laughed at by my mother and father if I wanted to turn away or leave the room. I would hear, "Oh, look at the baby over there!", followed by chuckling. I was also threatened with, "Don't take your eyes off of it. You'd better learn what you're supposed to do!" when watching it. Watching these films was my homework, and my parents expected results. I was supposed to be able to duplicate what I was seeing to a "T". I wonder if the adult pornography industry knows that its products are being used every day to train small children on how to be raped.

The worst form of manipulation I was forced to swallow, however, was when I was forced to watch snuff films. If you aren't sure what snuff films are, they are movies where children perform sexual acts on film and are murdered afterwards. Can you imagine? I couldn't do anything but follow their demands, please the customers, and do it without a single tear in my eyes.

We need to protect our children from these tactics. We need to watch, not with paranoia, but with instinct and an educated eye, to safeguard the innocence of the children in our care, whether they're our patients, our students, our neighbors, or our children.

LETTER TO MY NAMELESS ABUSERS

Nameless abusers,

    I see you. There is no doubt that I see you every day. But one day, I won't. One day you'll fade into nothingness. On most days, I know that my parents trafficked me, and you were clients that they found to strip me of myself, and fatten their purse strings - but this letter isn't for them. It is solely for you.

    When I was a small child, and teenager, I would see you attacking me out of thin air. I could see you not only in my nightmares, but while I was awake. I would be walking through the halls at school, and all of a sudden I would think that one of you was running at me and grabbing me. You, with the shoulder length brown hair, a blue button-down shirt, and khaki pants, came at me so often. People must've thought I was crazy as I swatted back at you or ran in another direction. I would run with heavy, halting breath, only to look back and see nothing chasing me, and no hands gripping my biceps.

    I have clumped all of you into one monster. You're like an evil Transformer in my mind's eye. You separate and attack when you want to. It seems I have no control over it right now, but I'm working on it. One day, you will be but a whisper in my life instead of the heavy metal guitar solo I am forced to listen to right now.

    I don't know where to begin with how ANGRY I am at you for abusing me, for threatening me with more bodily harm, and for threatening that my dad would lose his job and our family would be out on the street if I told anyone about the abuse. I know there is a stronger word than anger, but I don't know what it is. I have such a hard time connecting with my anger, but I've connected with it just fine for you.

    You made me feel responsible. Responsible for the safety and well-being of my family, and for what you stripped from me.

    I do wish I could remember your names. I wish I could write your names on individual pieces of paper and burn them. I want to watch *them burn and disappear into ashes. I want the ashes to rise so that the wind can deal with you. I want you to burn and then dissipate in the air so that you can evaporate into nothingness like you burned away my self-esteem, sense of self, and purity.*

But now, you no longer have control over me. I will win this war of torture and peace. Just you watch... I will win! Or better yet, don't watch. Don't be concerned with me. I don't need the threat of having you around while I heal. I don't need the threat of you to fight against because I'm already free.

I'm freeeeeeeee!

-Adira

Collage

Am I just a smudge?
A hint of black streaking
Little thumbprints across a canvas of
Blues, greens, and pinks?

A picture of all that I am
hides in the purples,
the brightest purples.

But it's smudged.
Unclear.

What does my life really look like
Below the blurs and the blank spots?

The first layer of color was my birth
and first year.
Pinks and baby blues.

The rest of my childhood shrouded in a haze
that layered upon layer upon layer of dark hues.

Until now.

What is there now but color peeking out of
trauma's dense fog of pain and sadness?
Are midnights and smokey greys all I will see
from now on?

I feel numb, like a mask that covers

The colors of my life.

But there is a collage still
Underneath it all
A collage of colors as bright as anyone else's

Yellows, oranges, and reds.

LETTER TO MY FACELESS ABUSERS

Faceless abusers,

    It is so strange to talk to you without having a face to imagine, or a name to attach, but I have felt you for so long. I have felt your bodies pressing on mine, your lips sloppily covering my tiny lips, your strong hands on my limbs, and the look and feel of the clothing you wore. I have felt your evil for so long, and I am ready to pry you off of me.

    I remember seeing you, the man that buried me up to my neck for urinating on you during the abuse you inflicted on me. I remember you dragging me down the stairs and out the back door, carrying me to the side of my garage, and accepting the shovel from my mother What time of day was it? I can't make that out, but it's time for you to get off of me now. To get out of my head. To get away from my body and my thoughts.

    You, the man that threatened to hang me if I told anyone about you. I haven't forgotten about you either. I will never forget walking with you past that beautiful dog hanging off of the tree trunk down the street from the house you abused me in, and being told that I could meet the same fate. I was understandably horrified! It was horrible enough without any personal connection, but that dog looked just like my best childhood friend that had passed away, which was my German Shepherd named Shasta. Whatever injustice caused the dog to be hanging to its death, I felt for him, I felt for his owners, and I felt like bawling. I remember your lips forming the words, "Don't tell anyone about this or me or that will be you". I remember your greasy brown hair that turned lighter around your face, your tanned hands and chest, and your white button-down shirt that your chest hair escaped from. I can't see your cheeks, or chin, but I can see your eyes - the windows into your evil soul. The abuse you repeatedly exacted on me physically, sexually, and mentally, haunted me for years, and I remember it like it happened yesterday. I'm releasing you *now.*

I release both of you, and all of the other faceless men that were among the dozens and dozens of abusers that took the baton from my mom and dad, and stole more of my childhood. You will always be a fact in my life, but I release your control over me.

In fact, I ban you from me.

You don't deserve to have any of me... not then, and not now.

With that, I release my hatred so that I can welcome more peace into my life without you.

-Adira

Hope

Hope is my fickle love.
He runs and hides without warning,
And then rushes back to hold me,
Care for me,
Caress me.

His coquettish ways
Draw me into him, but he knows just
What to do to crush me and my dreams
With one disappearing act.

Like an unstable rock on the side of a mountain,
Hope looks so bold and solid and true,
But he can come tumbling down with the
Slightest shimmy of what lies beneath.

Fitful and unsettled,
Hope tries to break my heart,
But I still long for him,
I still believe in him,
And I still swoon under his gaze.

Sometimes I feel foolish for believing in hope,
But I can't stop trying to hold onto his hand,
And dance with him until faith is born.

COPING WITH EXPRESSIONS OF TRAUMA

I want to name some of the expressions of trauma that I regularly experience, and give examples of useful ways to cope with them. Different expressions of trauma include, but are not limited to: dissociation, anxiety, hyperarousal, hypervigilance, flashbacks, self-harm, night terrors, chronic physical health issues, avoidance and isolation, difficulty trusting, and grieving your trauma - which can look like anger, fear, or sadness to name a few.

Scent -

Scent is the sense with the strongest connection to memory, both in a positive and a negative way. I have found that carrying a rollerball perfume of a scent that I connect positively to can help ground me. Using a scented oil in a sponge that is enclosed in a pendant can have the same effect. If I can catch myself when I am starting to feel like I'm dissociating, I use the rollerball, or simply bring the pendant to my nose and it has really helped me come back to the present moment. I've also put scented sachets in my pillow case to help me sleep a better, and to smell after I come back from a flashback or night terror in bed. Trying to connect a smell to relaxation and centeredness and using it to overpower the trauma response when triggered is so important. But, don't just use scent as a tool for the after effects of a flashback or episode of crippling fear. If you practice using this and other techniques when you are grounded, you can create pathways in your brain that connect the scents to being okay in the present moment. This can make the return to the present moment both easier and quicker, and it can also keep you centered for a longer period of time.

Scented putty –

Scented putty can combine the power of scent with the sense of touch. I have a lavender scented putty that I carry with me in my purse as well. It's in a silver tin, so it stays fresh and clean, and I pull it out especially when I'm feeling anxious. I take it out and knead it in my hand, which brings me back to the present moment on two fronts (touch and scent). It is also great that the lavender scent stays on my hand after I've used the technique, so I can utilize its gifts over and over.

Movement -

I use movement to help regulate my emotions all the time, whether it's walking around in my house, swaying to music, doing some chair yoga, or taking an excursion outside to immerse myself in the grounding power of nature. I'm disabled, but you can also include dancing, hiking, or using a more strenuous workout as tools in your toolbelt as well. Moving has been proven to be an important way to get in touch with your body which is where so much of our trauma is stored. It can help connect you to your present and understand your past. As my body experiences and expresses itself through movement, it is interpreting and interacting with my trauma. Without any words spoken, the processing begins.

In fact, renowned psychiatrist Bessel van der Kolk said in a The New York Times interview that "trauma has nothing whatsoever to do with cognition," he says. "It has to do with your body being reset to interpret the world as a dangerous place." Furthermore, he said, "The single most important issue for traumatized people is to find a sense of safety in their bodies."[8] Personally, I have found that combining simple movement with focused breathing has been an extraordinary way for me to regulate my emotions and find safety in my body both from my past and my present.

Journaling and artwork -

Journaling and artwork are also wonderful techniques I've used to cope with expressions of my trauma. These techniques allow me to write out my feelings and highlight the senses that have been activated by these expressions. I can also use paint, pencils, or fabric to express them through a visual media. I also practice my breathing while I'm doing it so that I can reset from whatever has pulled me off of my center.

Journaling and creating art also give me a moment to let fears, feelings of hurt, or feelings of hurting myself pass. Because I suffer from suicidal ideations and self-mutilation, I focus on another breath being another moment to make a good choice. Instead of saying "I'm going to cut myself instead of kill myself", I am able to make a choice to write in my journal, reach out to a friend, or pull out my paints to thrash on paper instead of thrashing myself.

Please remember that another breathe is another moment to make a good choice and please take care of yourself.
You are worthy!

Writing

Writing saved me on so many levels, and it still does. Being able to express myself on paper has always felt very freeing. I kept a few diaries growing up, which helped me with the actual skill of writing, but I remember not feeling safe to say what I felt for fear of my parents or brother reading it.

I do remember writing a story in second grade called "Rainbow Land" which won an award. I also wrote a story about my teeth that was published in the Detroit News as a fifth grader. My dental health was atrocious because of malnutrition and because I had a disease that settled in my gums when I was 3 years old that caused me to have a 104.7 degree fever and affected my adult teeth. I described the way my teeth looked like broken eggs, and how much I was bullied for it. I now think of the article as my first mini memoir. I was able to express my pain, and showed amazing resilience at such a young age. Using writing as a positive coping mechanism, I told the world what I was going through.

Expressing myself through poetry felt both like protection, and an avenue for my soul to talk. I learned about poetry as an elementary school student, and I latched onto it right away. It took me a while to figure out that I could also write that way, but by middle school I started to write in stanzas, and tried to convey my feelings fully using the fewest words possible.

Journaling is a very powerful and positive coping mechanism that I use now as well. I tend to do stream of consciousness writing in my journal, so I don't think the entries make very much sense to anyone except me. However, you can certainly write with purpose in many ways. You can write poetry, stories, and record your daily life in endless ways. Do what feels right to you. The important thing is that you are using it to express yourself.

You can yell in a journal, make holes in it, or make rainbows of hope with your words. It's the perfect format to be intentional with your thoughts and feelings. It is a place where you can take risks to express yourself, and journaling can be a tremendous source of stress relief because of that. It is also an amazing way to later self-reflect on what you have written and how you were feeling at a particular time in your life. There are so many times that I'm surprised at what comes out of me when I just allow myself to write without rules or boundaries. You can reflect and honestly get to know yourself on another level.

I've seen people incorporate their artwork into their journal writings as well, which combines two coping mechanisms. I've seen people make the paper in their journals by painting, cutting and pasting bits of paper together. I've also seen others collage pictures like mini dream boards and staple them into a notebook that they write in. Visually, this can be very powerful. There are endless opportunities to make your journal your own, and they can be as private as you want them to be.

As you get more comfortable with conveying yourself in this format, you may find yourself not only enjoying a level of stress relief, but you will start to gain a better insight into yourself, your needs, your accomplishments, and your dreams. With that new found knowledge, you can start to feel lighter and happier.

I only wish happiness for you!

THE BALLOON STORY

One day I was in a balloon.
It was a beautiful sunset.
I saw a kitten walking around.
The sun was so beautiful I cude not get over it.
If you went in a balloon you would think it was too!

-Written by me in second grade

LIBRARY IS FUN

What I want to do when I grow up!!!!

By Adira James in 2nd Grade

When I grow up I
want to be a artist
because I love drawing
and paint. I like watching other
people draw too. I like watching
Dena draw a lot. I will go to art school to learn.

How to Draw a Pirson

By Adira James

First you get a peace of paper and a pencil. Then you draw a circle, then you make a little half circle about an inch away from the bottom of your circle, if your makeing a big picture. Then you make a circle the other way around, but make it alot smaller. Then you make two little dots on the face a little higher then the nose. Then you make hair on top of you head. Then you make arms. A little down the face you make two line on each side one under the other. Then you make hands at he end of the arm. Then you make a circle under the middle of the arms. Then you make two little lines again one next too the other. Then you make little shoes under the legs.

-Written by me in Second Grade

Art

Art has been an amazing coping mechanism throughout my entire life. When I was a child, my dad would bring home scrap paper home from work, and I would staple them together to make little books. I first created stories with just pictures. Then, by the age of three, I was creating with both words and images. I remember being shut in my closet, and hiding under my clothing with one of these homemade blank books, and creating a story about turkeys around Thanksgiving. I created a story about Native Americans gathering and hunting a turkey for dinner. I added colorful feathers on the people's heads, added sharp pointed arrows, and the turkeys had brightly colored feathers as well. I even created structures behind the hunting scene to create depth, all with my instincts.

When I look back on it now, and it is amazing what I was able to create as a preschooler. I didn't have the ability to spell properly, but my basic syntax was correct. This showed how intently I listened - for yelling, for my parents plotting, and for my directions on what to do with a client both from my parents and from the clients themselves.

My trauma brain was well trained to use art as an escape from what was going on in my everyday life. As a teenager I practically lived in my school's art room. I was there every second that I wasn't in another class, including lunch time. I created collages, pieces painted with tiny dots, sculptures, and photographs. I don't think that I had a favorite outlet, but I remember the meticulous nature of the dot paintings being particularly satisfying. To break down the subject into tiny parts and then put it back together as a portrait mirrored my feelings about myself – a person made of tiny broken parts that was put together in a way that made sense from a distance. If you looked at me close-up, however, I was still in pieces. I felt so broken as a teenager that it didn't take a leap to feel my intense anxiety or connect with my suicidal ideations. I didn't think that I would ever be a whole person because of what I went through. I Making these pieces of art helped me feel a wholeness on some level since I was making something else whole.

Escaping through creation is such a powerful way to cope with difficult triggers and trigger responses. Creating is a space to express yourself on a new plane. For me it is a place to express my emotions and make sense of the things I am struggling with. Others may feel that art is a place to create boundaries and solidity out of the chaos inside. However art fuels you, I feel everyone can benefit from utilizing its powers and its grace. Whatever you create is right. There is no wrong. It is as welcoming as Mother Earth. It can take your triggers, your chaos, and your fears and turn them into understanding and comfort.

When I was at my most recent drug and trauma rehabilitation center, I followed suit with the teenager inside of me, and I practically lived in the art therapy room. I was there in between my sessions and classes, I ate my meals in there, and I finished my night in there. It was my safe haven. I did quite a few projects, from painting canvases and writing poetry on them, to making magazine collages.

One of the powerful exercises was making a mask. On the front side was the image of what I wish I saw in myself, and the back of it showed the descriptors of that reality. Then I made another mask of what I truly felt about myself in the present moment, with the back filled with words of how I felt in my current reality. Both masks brought up so much emotion. I painted my positive mask green and did a collage of flowers on it to show the life and future that was inside of me. The masks filled with pain showed an image of me lost in a fog of darkness. As I look at both of them now, I am filled with so much more emotion than I thought that I would be. Some of the descriptors I put on the backs of each of the masks I feel are true now. I feel like I am courageous, inspired and inspiring. I also take positive risks, and I feel that I am able to hold space for others to connect. At the same time, I still feel lost, depressed, disjointed, and somewhat broken. I can only be thankful that I am a hybrid of my past feelings and my future feelings. I feel worthy of the positives, I just need to feel them as present moment emotions and truths. I will get there, and if you're struggling, so can you.

While I was at this particular rehab center, there was another assignment I was given by one of my therapists which was to make a trauma egg. I painted my egg on a canvas. Inside the egg is cracked pieces that I labeled with my traumas including, incest, pain, stalked, buried, and abortion. On the sides of the egg are four lists. Under "mom" I wrote what roles she played in my trauma such as narcissist, liar, drunk, madame, and tormenter. On the other side were my dad's roles. I described him as a rapist, boss, drunk, groomer and more. On the bottom were house rules that I had to follow, like "go with whoever whenever, and obey or be beaten" and my roles that I played within the trauma, including slave, currency, and caretaker. It was beyond powerful to see all the cracked shards of trauma. When I broke it down, it was shocking to see how many of them there were and to see the roles my parents really played in my trauma when I wasn't holding back, making excuses, or utilizing the power of avoidance.

Another one of the most powerful exercises we were given at the rehab was making a body map. We were given a 6ft x 3 or 4ft piece of butcher paper and one of the other patients traced my body on it. The exercise was to write on it and paint it with how you feel about yourself, the damage that was done to you from your trauma, and what you feel others see you as. Scary, right? It was petrifying to start it, but as I kept going, I felt more empowered writing everything out even though it made me cry and purge so many awful emotions. I decided to lay on my sheet with my arms in prayer above my head and my feet apart. I chose this pose because I wanted to show my wrists tied together and my legs open for the abuse to follow. That was a position I was put in many times for clients as a child. Just writing this and thinking of my body map is giving me the chills. It was very powerful to depict myself with dark hues and red cuts of blood as I painted words like broken, fear, slave, and property around my frame.

Right now, I have tears coming to the surface of my eyes just like I did when I was making it. Now my tears are brimming and overflowing like a Greek vase. I am crying with this piece of art, with me in art therapy, and with me as the child in a woman's body that I was depicting. I am crying just like it is overflowing off the body map with pain. If you choose to do this project, you can destroy the map to symbolically release your attachment to it. However, I kept mine to remind myself how far I have come, and to help me continue releasing the pain when I need to.

After completing this piece, I was so moved by the process of showing all of this pain in two-dimensional art, that I decided to make a second map showing how I *want* to feel about myself. Out of this map came hope. Out of this map came courage. Out of this map came love for myself. It was so compelling to see myself as a powerful woman. I didn't have as many words to describe myself because it was foreign to think positively about myself, but as I placed labels of strength on my image, a phoenix began to appear in my mind's eye. I actually painted myself without a mouth or any other facial markers apart from my eyes because I could see my potential, but I didn't have the voice yet to express it. I was a phoenix rising from the ashes of my childhood. Much like I feel the Littles kept light shining within us regardless of the torture we were victims of, I felt that the strength within me had allowed me to rise above the ashes of despair I had been sitting in. I have to remember to keep this phoenix body map nearby so that I can look at it when I feel worthless, immensely depressed or suicidal.

One of the things that I learned from my body map experience is to try to balance out the heaviness of my expressions with the lightness of hope and future realizations even if I don't quite believe them to be true yet. Much like affirmations, focusing on art as a way to attract present moment happiness is a very therapeutic way to invite positivity into your life. I sometimes spend a day doing paint splatter with bright colors, work on a weaving project with pastels, or take pictures of a sunrise or sunset and revel in its beauty.

There are so many forms of art. Just keep trying until you find one or two that you feel an affinity towards, then allow yourself to soak in their beauty and their gifts.

Art can be medicine if we let it nourish us!

A Work in Progress

Sometimes I feel like my trauma
Is covering me devouring me
With a thick bumpy layer of papier-mache.

With this solid mask, I feel like I AM my trauma,

But I'm not.

My past pain is a part of me
Like a messy first grade art project.

Trauma has molded much of what I am,
But I am not my past.

I know that if I allow myself
to disintegrate under this mask
All of my dreams will be ravaged
Like my body was as a child.

I can't let that happen. I won't.

I have to let my light pierce through
The heaviness,
Focusing my energy
On comforting the parts of myself
That endured so much.

Underneath this mask is a woman.
A complicated, shapely, artistic woman.

A work in progress.

Art Therapy Images

SUNBEAMS THROUGH BLANKETS | 111

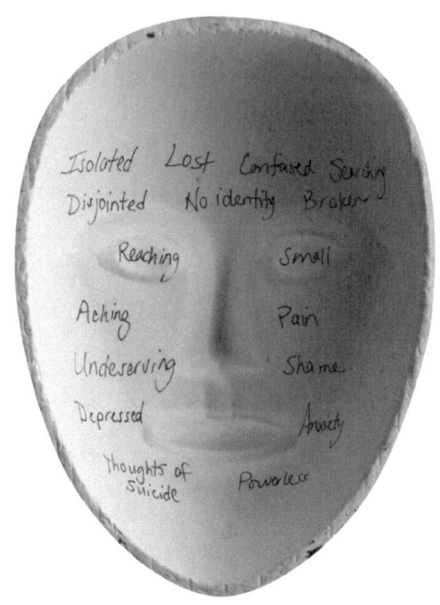

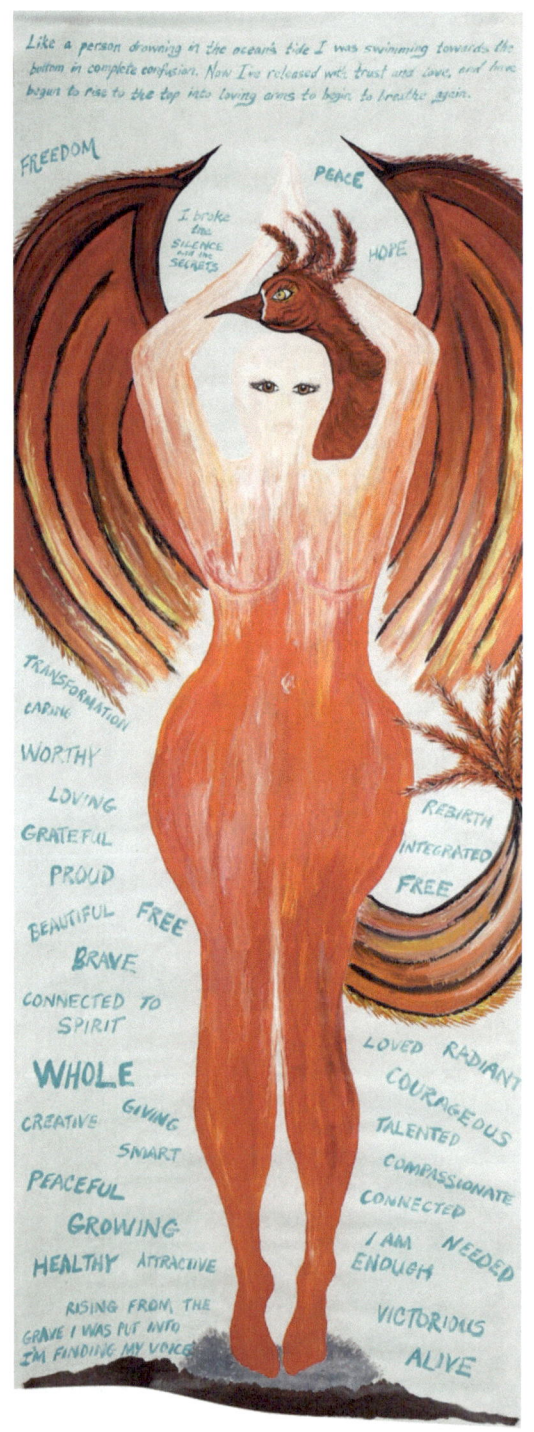

To Brush and Sweep

The paint dripping off my brushes
Falling pink
   Red
   Orange
     Orange-Yellow
   Dots
Swirling together.
Making a sunset come alive
over the River's
Reflection.
Blue
   Blue-Green
     Brown
Grey
The reeds coming up from the water
Green
   Green-yellow
     Lime
       Straw

I feel so alive when I paint.
To connect with the ethereal.
To try to capture what cannot possibly be
Captured.
To show what freedom is,
   What hope is,
     What life finding a way is.

To paint and sweep
Colors that are beyond my imagination,
Beyond what seems possible,
But shows up on paper and canvases and walls.

To bring life to the blank
To slither around the canvas like the paint on my fingers

To feel.

To allow my body to rest while my intuition works.
To connect my body and mind and heart in synchronicity
as I slide my vision onto a singular object and
have that be enough.

Maybe I'm enough.

I AM.

Splatter

Princess

Looking at my childhood drawing of a princess or ballerina, I immediately see a sad face on her belly. It's right there in front of me. The only way I could communicate that I was being abused as a child was through my artwork. There's a sad face on her abdomen, right in the spot where I was being abused. Seeing it is just heart wrenching for me. It's devastating to see the pain that four or five-year-old me delt with and was desperately trying to express. It brings me to tears.

As I look at the drawing, tears fall down my cheeks like a winding river, hugging to my face, jaw, and neck. I don't even have the energy to wipe them away or grab a tissue. I'm just falling. Falling into a pit of "why?" So, I try to focus on the rest of the drawing. I see the beige paper it's drawn on - at least it's beige now with time and sitting in a box in a basement for forty years.

When you look at the drawing, you see that the little girl is smiling. She wears long side pigtails and has a baby blue crown that matches her dress. There seem to be sparkles on her dress, and there is lace on the edge of the bottom of the dress and the short sleeves. She carries some kind of a trumpet, or horn, and has one bent leg facing the base leg's knee like a ballerina doing a passe. She has black stockings on and pink slippers with little knots on top. She's an adorable little princess.

Then you see the dark face with dark pigtails on her abdomen and going down the skirt portion of her dress.

I wonder if any teachers saw this drawing and thought about the possibility that something might be wrong in my household, or if they just thought I'd drawn a sad ballerina or princess. I'm not even sure if I drew it in class or if I drew it at home. If it was drawn at home, I know it fell on unfocussed eyes and deaf ears.

My drawing truly showed the pain and sadness I was feeling in my little womb while trying to smile to the outside world. What a brave little girl I was to try to express that. I was doing art therapy all on my own.

Seeing this drawing makes me want justice for her and for us even more. It makes me want to try to come out from under the blankets.I love you little one!

Princess

LONELY

By Adira James

*I was lonely when
Seema and Dena were
Playing together and Ali
Was playing with Becky,
Lisa, Linda, and Stephanie.
So I was left alone under
The tree. I was sad indeed.*

-Written by me in Second Grade

Friends

MOVIES

Untitled

Fortunately, I love you.
Unfortunately, you don't like me.
Fortunately, I love birthday parties.
Unfortunately, no one invites me except one person...
And that's me.
Fortunately, I got to play on the Jungle Jim.
Unfortunately, no one likes to play with me.

-written when I was 7 years old for a First Grade project

Containment Bowl

Containment is a wonderful coping mechanism if you are having a rush of overwhelming emotions and don't know where to put it all. I have used it regularly after I have flashbacks – which occur several times a day. I often get overpowered with grief, sadness, confusion, and anxiety as a fallout from these flashbacks, and I simply don't know what to do with it all and still be able to function. I use the containment mechanism to take the volume of emotion that I can't process when I come out of the flashback, and put it in a literal or figurative box, bowl, or any container I can think of.

I let the emotions sit in there while I gather myself up. I embrace all of my dissociated parts that have been affected by the flashback, and when I am ready, centered, and focused, I peel open the container and start to process it. If I am unable to do that alone, I process my emotions in my therapy sessions where I can be guided through the container.

I recently made a containment bowl in art therapy that I have begun to use daily. I used papier-mache to create the structure of the bowl, and I painted the outside to resemble a bird's nest. I lined the top of the bowl with large stiff feathers to protect my thoughts. Then, I painted the inside of the bowl like a river bed and put soft baby feathers inside so that my emotions could have a safe landing.

Making this bowl was richly rewarding. I didn't think about what I was going to do before I did it. After I made the bowl's structure, I let it evolve organically. Making it helped me envision the place where I want my emotions to go while I bring myself back to present moment.

It amazed me that I wanted to put my emotions in a river with a basket of soft baby feathers. It is really lovely. I always see a river as a wonderful way to think of time and energy. Every time you step into a river, it's a new river because the water flows, circles, and passes you by. It is a perfect example of the present moment. Putting the river inside of my containment bowl is such a great choice. My emotions are like the river, always evolving as my circumstances change. In this example of containment, letting my thoughts sit in the river helps me process them before I start to focus on them. I am allowing my emotions to evolve on their own to a place closer to the present moment, and only then am I focused on resolving them.

I am so thankful that my therapist assigned me the task of making this bowl. It truly has brought me to a new level of understanding of myself and my emotions. It is yet another arrow in my quiver for coping with my trauma.

Nest Bowl

CHOCOLATE

Crunchy chocolate cut by my teeth
like a lawnmower.

Shreds slide down my throat
I swallow with glee bite after bite.

Hungry for bliss
I swallow bite after bite with desperation.

Will it collect at my hips
Or thighs?

At least it won't slither down my throat
And live in my liver

Like the pure joy
of a bottle of bourbon.

Maladaptive Coping Skills

I hated myself for so many years because of the way I was raised in the midst of predators. Being sex trafficked, I was used as a tool for others' pleasure. I didn't have support as a human being from my parents, and it left me with destructive ideas that would end me slowly but surely. I used unhealthy coping skills like they were my best friend and my savior because they at least kept me alive. I cut myself, drank and did drugs, choked myself, starved myself, and did so many other things that hurt my body, my heart, and my soul.

Cutting myself as an alternative to committing suicide is like making a bargain with myself, "I will endure the pain of this cut, and it will be enough to keep me alive." I have gone to the hospital when I have felt suicidal beyond just ideations, and please be sure that you do too.

Asking for help is a strength.

It's what warriors do.

As much as I knew cutting, drinking, and many of my other techniques were destructive, it was as if I couldn't see any other way to cope. It was like going to the path of least resistance. I had used many of these negative mechanisms as a programmed response to stress throughout my childhood and adulthood. The hardest thing for me is to change the neuropathways that lead me directly to the negative behavior, and create new ones that lead me on a healthier path. That is what I am trying to master now, and it is making a huge difference in my life.

If I do fall into a negative groove of using maladaptive coping skill, I try to immediately make a choice to follow it with a positive coping skill to regain that balance again. Following through with the positive can be very scary because it is foreign, and change is scary. I have used the unhelpful for far longer than the new techniques I am trying to master now.

Even though I don't look at my old coping skills as my best friend anymore, I do honor them now because they helped me survive when I was at my most vulnerable. I see that they're maladaptive, not just coping skills. I now know that there are many more positive options to get me through the day and to catapult me to the other side of a trauma trigger or flashback. I am in a place now where I can see that I am no longer a child who is a victim of slavery anymore. I am an adult in full control of my life, and I can choose to make loving decisions for myself.

I will discuss many more positive coping skills that can immediately ground you and move you past your trigger response in the chapters to follow, such as using ice in your hand, gently snapping a rubber band on your wrist, or using your favorite scent on a piece of cloth in a locket. Also, I will talk about how you can use breathing, yoga, cooking, music, and gardening to move yourself out of a trauma response and into a new space of centeredness, peace and joy.

I'm going to continue to show you how I've used these techniques, and how they have helped me in my own life. We all have trauma that we deal with, and I hope you can experiment with these positive coping skills in order to find more peace in your life as well.

We all deserve happiness and joy!

SHAKEN

Me and my bottle.
Shaken
Stirred
Swirled
every day and night.

I gave this brown elixir
back to the bartender
with a look of desperation.
Tangled inside.

Flustered, she looked back with
surprise
I had only ever asked for more,
so she asked me if I was sure.

At the same time, pills were melting in my hand.
Gems that kept my voices at bay,
and welcomed my heart beating loudly in my ear.

I threw away the handful
that had mounded in my hand.
It was waiting to give me Heavenly peace
for now, and forever.

As I watched them tumble
into the bag like a board game,
making it around the other pieces of trash
until they trickled to the bottom.

I realized that now I was dry.
Parched.
Empty.

Free.

THE FLOOR

I woke up on the cool bathroom floor again. This time I was naked instead of half dressed, and my hips were curled into my chest – brown sugar against the creamy tile my husband chose. I turned my head to the left and right to ground myself in the moment, and I thanked goodness that I was in my bathroom instead of a stranger's. I crawled like a baby to the toilet seat and pushed myself up into an awkward, bent over position, and finally I slid my hands over to the white sink basin and used it to aid in pulling myself upright.

I didn't want to look in the mirror that was staring back at me, but I needed to assess any damage that I had done to myself the night before while I was blacked out. What I saw should've convinced me to stop drinking. I had a ring of last night's consumption around my lips, my eyes were dark and sunken in, my cheeks were feverish, and I saw a few new bruises on my right shoulder and hip, probably from when I fell to the ground. My hair was a nest of curls as wild as a squirrel's nest. I swirled some mouthwash in my mouth, and snap, crackle, popped my joints into submission.

I looked down at my feet and swayed back and forth with relief when I discovered my clothes were pushed against the bathroom door. I shook them out, and found there wasn't any foul smell attached to them, so I could put them on before I opened the door. I tiptoed back to my bed, and hoped that my husband didn't know how badly I indulged in the devil as I slowed my breath to his pace, and tried to go back to sleep.

That was not the final breaking point that pushed me into getting sober. What convinced me to go to rehab wasn't such an ugly moment. In fact, it was much quieter inside and out. I was forty-three years old. I realized that I had never been sober.

As a control technique for their abuse, my parents and clients had made me addicted to drugs and alcohol as a toddler. I was given alcohol from beer to hard liquor regularly, and I was forced to take drugs daily in pill form, intravenously, or with shots in order to keep me compliant. I was even given chloroform to keep me from knowing where I was going when I was taken to clients' houses.

I never stopped drinking and doing drugs from toddler age forward. The realization just clicked one day. My therapist had told me that I was an addict, other people had told me, as well, but I just didn't want to see it. My trauma was so severe that I needed these substances to function in the world. I needed the aid of drugs and alcohol to propel me out of my body so that I didn't have to feel. That is one of the ways that I survived.

Using this maladaptive coping skill, I was able to live my life. It was easier to compartmentalize my past and my present, and it kept me from having to think past the next bottle or pill that I would consume in the future.

The bathroom floor didn't feel like a bad place for me compared to having to feel and process the emotions that sprang from being trafficked. When I was using, I was just glad that I was home, that I had a home, that I had a few friends, and that I had a relationship with someone I trusted. All of these things were foreign to me when I was a child.

Walking into a rehabilitation and trauma center the first time in 2019, was the best thing that I could've done to get sober and start addressing the underlying reasons for my addiction. The sobriety didn't stick the first time, but I went back to the same rehabilitation center a second time a year later and I was able to keep my promise to myself and stay sober for years. Without the tools to learn how to process my emotions and unpack my trauma, I would've just turned back to drugs and alcohol again. I stayed for five weeks, and left the facility with a clear head on a level I hadn't felt before – ever.

I realized that although substance abuse was a way of coping my entire life, it was pushed upon me as a child and it wasn't my choice then. It helped me more easily endure the trafficking and all that came with it, and I truly honor its place in my life, but I no longer need it. Now, I have a loving husband, a beautiful home, a vehicle to take me places, and I live in a peaceful community where I can thrive. I've been given these gifts, and I realize that by using, I will only sabotage what I have been given and what I fight to foster in my life every day - happiness.

So, no more bathroom floors, and no more wondering where I am or where I have been for the past eight hours because of a chemical intervention. I am forced to cope healthily, to be an adult, and to make decisions that are best for me and my body.

It's not easy, but I am doing it one breath at a time.

THE BODEGA

Turn the corner
Wet crags.
Trip, trip, tripping,
Falling
Under the spell of the night.

Bright neon
Apple green.
Pulse, pulse, pulsing,
Vibrating
With the hum of the light.

I read the sign Bodega
B
O
D
E
G
A

Elephant leaves
Green-Yellow
Drip, drip, dripping,
Sweating
Kissing the window
Or trying to escape.

I join the leaves
From the other side

Fingers slide, slide, sliding
Clawing to get in for my drink
But I know it's a mistake.

No one is home, but
The leaves
The sweat
The light
The broken sidewalk

There I
Fall, fall, keep falling,
At the threshold.
Waiting for
The sign to say open again.

CRUMBLING

I feel like I'm collapsing
After I trip
On the corner of the rug.

I can't seem to hold my head up,
I nod and nod.

Crumbling,
As I slip on wet stairs and go
Summersaulting down to the sea.

Sinking below the surface of the water
I succumb to its rhythm and wisdom.

Bobbing up to air and back down to the depths
I roll into and out of the tide.

How many pills did I take this time?

Falling

Because I was forced to use substances so early on, along with the fact that both of my parents were alcoholics, I don't feel I truly had a chance to avoid being an addict. Not only was it seemingly an impossible task to stay sober, but I had no idea how to feel or process emotions successfully. I had been in the habit of drinking until I blacked out, or taking pills to float away from the experiences in my life. I never allowed myself to fully feel happy, sad, or anything in between. It was just more palatable to live my life in a fog and not allow my body or my mind to remember all of the abuse that I had endured during and after I was sex trafficked. I also didn't think that I deserved to feel the happiness that was in my life. I turned all of the shame and anger that I had bottled inside from my past in on myself instead of allowing myself to appreciate the joy.

Being sober from drugs and alcohol has opened up a new world to me, but it has been very confusing. I am not used to thinking with a sober brain. I have had to go through intensive therapy, rehab, and more intensive therapy to get to where I am, and still I slipped up and fell off the wagon of my alcohol and drug addiction several times before it stuck. One time I fell off the wagon only two days after I left the rehab. What broke my heart was when I had over two years of sober time and I succumbed to my drug addiction again. I was so proud of myself this time, counting the days on my calendar, and faithfully accepting my chips in awed by my inner strength.

Then I fell. I fell hard.

There was a very hard month last summer where I felt so hopeless day after day that I attempted suicide by drug overdose twice in one month. The suicide attempts were scary - not just for me, but also for my husband. It was horrible of me to attempt to end myself. He lost his mother that same month, and I can't imagine what it would've done to him if I was gone too.

He told me that I just slept for hours and hours with each

attempt. The first time, he thought that I was just sick, but then he realized that something was very wrong. He shook me over and over. Thank goodness my tolerance for drugs was so high from using for so long, because he eventually shook me awake. I was still under the influence, and I just remember seeing him like I was looking up from drowning in a slow-moving river. His face moved with the current, and I felt weightless. I felt like I was part of the current. He yelled at me, which sounded garbled and confusing, until I came to the surface and heard him clearly.

"What is wrong with you? What is going on? What did you take? Did you take your medicine?"

His flurry of questions both confused me, and brought me back to some level of clarity - I where I was and who I was with.

The second attempt wasn't followed with questions. He knew what I did, and he said, "Wow, what a month I would be having if both of you died." He hung his head and left the room. I couldn't feel any lower, and he had every right to walk away for a bit. Then, he came back and embraced me tightly while I held onto him for dear life.

It was awful. I have no excuse. I only saw myself as a burden, and I thought he would be better off without me - but I was wrong. My mother's words thumped in my head, "He is going to leave you and you will be left all alone". My husband disagrees. He has always said that he wants to live with me and love me even in the next life. Thank goodness I lived and can see that now. The strength I received from my husband gave me the support I needed to continue on, and he gave me the grace to find out that I wasn't a burden to him. Now, I just have to keep reminding myself of that.

Once I recovered from the suicide attempts, it had torn me up so much mentally, physically, and emotionally, that I felt lost. One of the ways that it tore me up was the shame of losing the accomplishment of my sober time. It was as if the entire last two years of sober time was wiped away with those two attempts. Maybe it is because I commonly suffer from suicidal ideations, but it actually struck me down more than the actual suicide attempts. It took a very life-changing Narcotics Anonymous meeting for me to realize that no matter what, my sobriety doesn't go away. I have to start over with a new Day One, Two, and Three, but it doesn't take away the 903 days that I had worked so hard for. Realizing that saved me from a major relapse with the drugs and alcohol as well as a possible third suicide attempt. No matter what happens, my accomplishments don't go away. They're not erased with time.

The time and strength that I gained from therapy and all the hard work that I put into surviving every day gave me the energy I needed to wake up and keep trying to thrive. I know that I couldn't have chosen life each day from then forward without all of that hard work. All that I've learned doesn't get erased by falling down either.

In fact, nothing goes away. The abuse I suffered doesn't go away, but I can allow it to stay in the past. The feelings of shame I was programmed to feel about myself aren't gone, but they've softened and will continue to soften as my body and mind realize that I was trained to feel that way about myself as a child. I still have flashbacks about the trafficking, and I will continue to have triggers, but they will lessen as my body realizes that the abuse is not happening *now*. And the happiness and happy times I experienced before my suicide attempt didn't go away, they were just there to hug me when I came back to myself and realized that life is precious. Falling doesn't mean that I'm done.

I deserve to be here, and I can make an impact in this world.

If you are feeling suicidal,
Please call the National Suicide and Crisis Hotline at 988,
Call someone you trust,
Or please go to the hospital.
The world wouldn't be the same without you as a blessing!

DETOX

Dizzy and floating to the floor in agony.
Falling to the floor in actuality.

Sweat dripping,
slithering between my breasts

What's left of me?

Chills
Shaking
Skin hurting too badly to scratch my itch.

Parched with no alcohol.
Dehydrated from the drugs.

Bones pulling,
    yanking,
        grinding out of my skin.

Anxious and exhausted,
which will win before I pass out again?

An IV pumping who knows what to keep me alive.
In and out of consciousness.

Delirious to the sounds in the room
A clang
    clash
of trays.
A voice reverberating off of my skull,
    not entering my ears.

The crying
Is it me or someone else?
Crying
Me
I'm crying non-stop in my dreams,
in my wake.

Alive.
Am I?

Burden

One of my biggest triggers is feeling like a burden to my husband. When I feel like that, my fears are at a ten out of ten that he will leave me because of my mental disabilities, my mental health issues, and my substance use disorders. Labeling myself as a burden rips out all of my anchors to reality, and I tend to run towards my suicidal ideations and my need to self-harm.

Just last month, we were talking about him going out of town for a couple of weeks, and he asked me, "What are we going to do about you being home alone?" I responded that I would be fine on my own, and "I didn't need someone to watch over me."

The last time he went out of town on business, we had a friend sleep over just in case I dissociated and decided to drive, to turn on the stove, or to do countless other things that could result in me getting hurt or the house catching on fire. Having someone stay with me then was a relief in some respects, but it also brought up quite a bit of shame. I'm an adult, but I can't be trusted to be by myself for a couple of weeks? You can imagine that I felt like a child in an adult's body, an emotional wreck, and I truly felt mentally ill. Nobody said any of those things to me, and nobody made me feel inadequate on any level, but I created the narrative in my head, and I stuck to it for the entire two weeks., fighting with myself every moment.

"You are so sick, that you can't make it on your own."

"Who would want someone like you?"

"Just have one drink... he's not here, he'll never know"

"He doesn't *really* want you. He is going to come back and divorce you."

"Slit your wrists, just do it."

"Healthy? Yeah right. You are sick!"

"Just end it already!"

Despite the instructions from my inner voice to hurt myself while he was gone, by some miracle, I didn't cut myself, strangle myself, or attempt any of the other forms of self-harm that I usually go to when I feel deep shame. Thankfully, I made it through the couple of weeks without incident using the many coping techniques I had learned. I actually came out of the two weeks feeling empowered because I had made it through without acting out the instructions I was hearing in my head.

After a lot of contemplation, and surviving these times of intense shame and fear, I realize that I am making the decision for both myself and my husband whether I truly am a burden. I am tripping and tumbling into a realm of emotion without any evidence. Without the facts.

I'm still learning, because healing is definitely not a straight trajectory, but I'm starting to make real connections with the concept of following the evidence instead of following the emotion or thought. Thoughts can come and go, and feelings can come and go, but evidence is more concrete. Allowing myself to feel an emotion, or just watch an emotion pass through me, and then look at whether anything concrete matches this fleeting feeling has really helped me not get stuck in the sticky web of shame.

So, I asked my husband if he felt I was a burden. He said, "What are you talking about?" He not only didn't feel I was a burden, but he felt the question was out of the realm of possibility. He said, "That's way out in left field. Of course I don't think that." After he said that it was my job to internalize the facts and allow my fears and shame to dissipate like a ring of smoke.

It's not easy, but it's so important to allow yourself to face the facts of a situation instead depending on the raw emotion or the triggers that erupt from a situation. Only then will you gain the perspective of present moment truth. Only then will you be able to feel unconditional love for yourself.

My Husband's Eyes

*What drives my panic the most
these days,
is to be a burden to my loved ones.*

*As much as I try to
Breathe,
Meditate,
Paint, and
Take my meds on time,*

*I still float,
And struggle not to indulge in taboos.*

I am petrified that I am too much.

That me, the essence of me, is a strain.

A load that they don't wish to carry.

*I worry that I am taking up too much space
That my breath is too hot.
My sighs are too thick.
My lumbering gate is too heavy.*

*I am afraid that my floating spirit will rise so high
that I am unreachable,
Like a balloon escaping a child's hand.*

*I don't want to be anyone's hardship,
Or a hinderance for their dreams.*

I only want to be a source of joy,
A partner in life's adventures,
A light in their eyes.

Every day I look into my husband's eyes.

I search past the hazel hues that sway towards brown
And then green,

Hunting for a twinkle when he gazes at me.

Every day I thank all that is good that it's there.

Luminous, kind, and strong.

PIECES OF ME

My body battered and bruised day after day.

From my brother's love,
the sting of a fork in my arm.
The pain of a knife in my back.
The hole in my forehead that imploded
from the corner of a speaker
because I didn't want to watch Star Trek.

The clients' hands twisting at my arms.
My wrists wrangled into submission by a rope.
The heat burning my skin as I was plopped too close
to the radiator for hours.

My mother's swift hand
hard as a rock against my bottom.
Faster than I could run and hide.

My father's villainous strength.
Dislocating hips to keep me in place to abuse.
Dislocating shoulders to further his cause.

Then I battered myself.
The rip of a steak knife carving out my forearms and wrists.
Scissors nipping out pieces of my wrists and thighs.
Starving my body to 81 pounds.
Choking myself into submission.
Submission to my belief that I didn't deserve to be
Breathing, walking, living, loving.

What's left of me after all of that?
Pieces of me trying to bond together to make a person.
Searching for a wholeness that I've never felt before.

I'm almost there.
In the here and now.
As I breathe and walk and love,
I'm almost one.

But I've won.

Forgiveness

I'm working on forgiving myself. I am so hard on myself when it comes to making mistakes. I can be triggered to hate myself for something as significant as cutting myself, or something as insignificant as forgetting to record a television show. I have the same hatred for myself whether I've done something I should or shouldn't be sorry for. Often times, I want to be punished for an act by using self-mutilation or denying myself food. It's like I'm compelled to throw acts of hate towards myself.

Learning to give myself grace has been a difficult path for me, but I'm trying with all of my might to follow it. As a child, I was programmed as a child to hate myself regardless of the situation, and to punish myself or be prepared to be punished if I made mistakes large or small – especially when it came to the clients I serviced. I know I'm an adult now. It's just a struggle to convince the rest of me that I can act differently than I've been trained to act.

Trying to escape this viscous circle of punishment has been more than a challenge, but I'm up for it now. I feel like I have enough tools to conquer this hatred and forgive myself not only for my mistakes, but for how I'm treating myself. I feel like I have enough strength to give myself grace for using maladaptive coping skills as solutions to my problems knowing that I won't *always* be compelled to use them.

I want to forgive myself for using the negative coping skills I was taught to use past the expirations date of adulthood. I think it's just going to take the repetition of positive reactions to the issues I am faced with in order to change the hardened neuropathways that have led me to doom. I need to take a breath after I'm triggered and let all of my hard work in therapy take hold.

Inhale
Exhale
Listen...
Is this a fact or a thought?

Is there anything I should be sorry for?
How can I hug myself in this situation?
How can I give myself grace?
In what way can I thank and love myself now?
How can I thank the me who endured the pain of our past?
And know that it's going to be okay.

Distract - Pause - Plan

One of my therapists taught me an amazing tool that gives me time to maneuver around or through a situation when I have been triggered and am tempted to immediately use a maladaptive coping skill. She called this exercise Distract – Pause – Plan.

If I am triggered or have overwhelming feelings, first I try to **distract** myself from them. For me, that looks like drawing or painting, looking at my fish tank and spending time with my animals, watching television, making jewelry, and writing. If I am able to **pause**, I sit still, use relaxing breathing techniques, listen to music, meditate, take a nap, or rest in my bed or on the couch.

After I have distracted myself and/or paused, I can start to make a **plan**. I make a list of projects to complete, break down larger tasks to create smaller tasks, give myself a time limit for my emotions to take over me, reach out to my therapist if needed, and use my support system of my friends and my husband.

No matter which one of the distract, pause, or plan techniques work, I have learned to be curious and investigate how I actually feel, and what those feelings make me want to do. Being curious is a wonderful tool. It allows you to ask questions, answer those questions for yourself, and slow things down.

"Am I feeling triggered by a scent? And is the memory that is coming up related to the present moment?"

"Is the loud noise that is making me hypervigilant a threat to me in the here and now?"

"Is that person's body language or image currently threatening, or does it remind me of an abuser from my past?"

This questioning helps me come back to the present moment so that I'm not swallowed up by my past trauma.

It is also important to combat negative self-talk with what you are doing right. For example, I sometimes feel like I don't do anything that's worth anything… that I am a loser in life. I respond to those

feelings with statements like these:
- I am attending therapy regularly and am seeking help.
- I am attending all of my doctor appointments.
- I am eating every day.
- I am keeping up with .my hygiene
- I am taking care of my pets.
- I am doing what I can to take care of the household chores.
- I am taking my medication daily.
- T am trying to set goals and achieve them.
- I am the author of three published books.
- I am currently writing another memoir.
- I am giving back and making a difference.
- I am taking some moments to do things that I like to do.

Asking for what you need from your support system is also important – you're worth it, and would do the same for them. I can ask for what I need by making statements like these:
- I need you to just be here and listen.
- I want you to hold me/hug me - it helps me feel safe.
- I need you to let me vent my emotions and thoughts.
- I need us to talk this through, and I need you to help me find a solution.
- I need you to help me feel better right now.
- I need you to not judge me right now.

Learning to slow things down, ask yourself questions, and articulate what you need are three pillars of healing. They are three pillars that anyone can use to connect with themselves and the world around them.

SPIRITUAL GROWTH

Love
Serenity
Clarity

Dirt built up into mountains
from service to others,
a comforting home,
and healthy long-lasting relationships.

The mountains crescendo into snowcaps
filled with snowballs of inner peace,
peace of mind,
and sobriety.

Powdery white clouds of hope
hover
in balance
with mental,
    physical,
        and emotional health
fluttering above each peak.

As a river flows towards me
I step in with toes searching
for the bottom through the mud.
Legs enveloped in the rushing currant.
Arms reaching for the sun.

Every moment a new chance to become centered on my path.

Love
Serenity
Clarity

GROWTH

Integration

When talking about Dissociative Identity Disorder (DID), I want to start with a definition. According to the National Alliance on Mental Illness (NAMI), DID is a disorder "characterized by alternating between multiple identities. A person may feel like one or more voices are trying to take control in their head. Often these identities may have unique names, characteristics, mannerisms and voices. People with DID will experience gaps in memory of every day events, personal information, and trauma." The organization goes on to say that, "dissociative disorders usually develop as a way of dealing with trauma. Dissociative disorders most often form in children exposed to long-term physical, sexual or emotional abuse."[9]

I found great comfort in these definitions and observations when I was researching the diagnosis I was given by my doctor and therapist gave me. Just like I did when I was introduced to the definitions of child sex trafficking, it encompassed everything that I was feeling and experiencing. I have chatter in my head constantly. I also lose time during the day when I dissociate, sometimes even to the point of driving somewhere and "waking up" in another place. I have even found myself walking outside in the frigid winter of Michigan barefoot in the snow when I should be in bed. Thank goodness my husband is a light sleeper and found me before I went too far.

It can be very upsetting for me to lose time, and it is sometimes impossible to think straight when I have four or five voices at a time talking or arguing in my head, but I have learned to accept it. I have learned that the Littles want to protect me like they did so many years ago, and they want to have a say in my daily activities – a luxury they didn't have when they embodied me decades ago- and that's okay. I have learned that as rigid as Emily is, she is trying to protect me. I have learned that Julia, though she is sometimes the voice that is trying to get me to kill myself, is in a space where she thinks I am still being trafficked, and she thinks there is no other way out. In her own way, she is trying to save me also.

Right now, as I'm writing, these are the voices I hear...

"Don't do this... don't talk about me!" says Emily "I said no, don't. you understand me?"

"It's for your own good." says Julia.

"I want cake! Didn't you say you were going to the market?" the ten-year-old exclaims.

"I want cake too!" several other voices chime in.

"Stop yelling" Emily says. "She needs to concentrate so she can finish writing and be done."

"I want cake!!!!!!"

I have at least eleven different parts that I know of. Eleven different beings that have opinions, actions, reactions, wants, and dreams, all living within me. To be honest, it can be exhausting, but it is also a privilege to give them a voice - especially the children. The children are pretty much always asking for food, especially tater tots with A LOT of ketchup, and chocolate vanilla marble cake. I was malnourished as a child, and that was all they knew before they separated from me at such young ages. I'm sure that's why they want to eat so badly now.

The children detached from me after traumatic events. For example, the baby probably separated after my first sexual abuse encounter, the five-year-old separated after the burial episode, and the ten-year-old separated after a particularly horrible beating followed by my parents tying me up in my closet. I don't know what all of the traumatic events were, but the alters are with me now. They are aware of each other, aware of me, and they are trying to communicate to feel safe.

There is a lot of focus and emphasis in the mental health world to attain full integration when it comes to DID. Integration for many means that you absorb the alters and they are no longer. There is a fragility to this concept, however, because as a person continues to deal from trauma, they may fracture again. For me, integration is not about eliminating these alters. It's about bringing all of my parts into my heart and loving them. I try to tell them over and over that I will take care of them no matter what, while I literally hug myself. I want to integrate the emotional aspects associated with the trauma that made them fracture off in the first place.

I also take care of them by buying stuffed toys and games that I keep in my office/art room for them to play with when they take over. When they are hungry and begging for tater tots, I start the tots in the oven, tell them they will be done soon, take them out of the oven, put them on a plate with the ketchup and then I step away and allow them to eat them. After they are done, I come back to the present moment me and clean up. They know that I have toys in my art room, so sometimes when I lose time, I find myself back on the floor in their playroom portion of my room playing with the dolls that I bought for them... dolls they weren't allowed to have when they were their present moment. The twenty-year-old, Emily, and the adult Julia don't ask for anything that I can hear, but just like any relationship, it is developing, and I'm sure that I will learn more about them as time goes by.

My main goal with integration is to keep myself in the driver's seat. I don't want anything dangerous to happen to me, so I try to remain two-headed with my alters so that I can hear them in my head, but I am in control. I want to only allow myself to lose time and allow them in the driver's seat if I am in a safe environment - like my home - with my husband nearby to monitor me. Over time, as I'm healing, I have seen a trend of them taking over less frequently. I feel like I'm gaining their trust, and they know that I love and respect them. I feel like they are starting to know that I am a responsible adult who can handle anything. I am a survivor just like them.

I have full faith that as I process and heal from my trauma, some of the alters will retreat because they won't feel that they need to protect me as much. They will feel that they aren't needed to hold space surrounding the intense issues I suffer from. I'm sure that they will come out to greet me, but will not take over at all.

I have never experienced life without the chatter of others in my head and in my heart. I don't expect, nor do I want, to shut them up and throw them out. We have survived together for almost a half century, and we have more memories to make.

We are warriors.

Through Her Eyes

One of the beautiful things about having fractured selves inside of me is my ability to see things through their eyes. Although it is truly a tragedy that I had to separate in order to survive, I have been given the amazing gift of being able to see wonder in the world like a child sees it. So many adults have to depend on the children in their lives to vicariously experience the world through their innocent eyes. I don't have to, and I am so grateful for that. It helps to counter the hurt and the ugliness that I feel and I experience every day as a result of the abuse.

I can see good in people and the world, and I think that's a miracle based on what I've endured. In my opinion, having the Littles (the me at young ages) inside giving me their input, is the only way that that could happen. Children are such amazing, resilient, and forgiving little beings. I don't think that I would be able to live in the world to the level that I do without their influence.

My stream of consciousness may not allow me to read very well, but I can see beauty in the mundane. My short-term memory is more than short, but I can look at a broken fence and see a woman's face. I lose time when disassociation takes the wheel, but I stop and take a picture of the sunrise every day, and talk to the animals that I encounter along the way. I sometimes have to be told, and reminded, and told again to do something, but I see the beauty in a tree that is growing out of a burned-out abandoned home. I can see life in the shadows, and I know that life finds a way.

Therapy

Talk therapy has been so helpful for me. Hearing myself talk and receiving expert advice has brought me another level of reality, consciousness, and understanding of myself, my situation, my past, and my present. From my late thirties on, I have been privileged to have had several therapists who have taken great care of me, and helped me grow as a person. Especially because I have Dissociative Identity Disorder (DID), and constantly have conversations going on in my mind, having someone guide me to a grounded state and help me to differentiate between the current reality and my past has been essential to my healing path.

Over the years, I have learned so much about myself, about my diagnoses, and about therapeutic techniques that have worked for me. One such nugget of knowledge is my Adverse Childhood Experience (ACE) score, a score that puts a numerical value on the abuse and neglect that a child has experienced or is experiencing. That number helps doctors and social workers identify the risk for damaging health problems as well as social and emotional problems a person may suffer from as an adult because of that abuse.[10] My ACE score is off the charts because of being trafficked by my family. Learning that has helped my therapists design the techniques they've used to help me, and my score has helped me understand why I am an addict, have so many health problems, have specific diagnoses, and so much more. It is amazing how being able to identify an issue makes it easier to combat - and helps you to have more grace for yourself as you do so.

Although I have learned so much more than I can discuss in this book, I wanted to introduce a couple of unique techniques that I have been helped me in combination with talk therapy. These techniques may also be helpful to others who are trying to better process their trauma.

Using a cue word is an interesting way to start changing your neuropathways so that your mind has a calm and centered response to a horrific memory or experience instead of having a response that is destructive to you – like physically hurting yourself. This technique is called Be Set Free Fast (BSFF) which was developed by clinical psychologist Larry Nims.

Your body is used to reacting to specific stimulus or triggers, in a certain way, and it has created programmed responses based on what has worked for you in the past. When you encounter a situation, your brain recognizes similarities to previous situations, and accesses the same response because it was previously successful. Not all of the behaviors that result from those neuropathways are healthy for you now though. For example, when I get anxious, quite often I want to hurt myself in some way, or perform some other maladaptive coping skill. Even though it wasn't healthy, it worked at the onset of my trauma to regulate my stress on some level. But I don't need to, or want to do that anymore. For example, if sexual contact was initiated, I would immediately start to float. I needed to dissociate in order to survive the situation as a five, six, twelve, and fifteen-year-old, but I am in my forties now, and married to a man who wouldn't hurt me. I don't need to float during sexual contact anymore.

Your cue word can be any word that you have a connection with. It could be as simple as "stone" or "sky". To start using your cue word to rebuild your neuropathways, there is a series of sentences you listen to your therapist say. You then respond with your cue word to begin the process of creating a break from old unhealthy patterns, and creating new ones that work in the present moment. After hearing and responding to these prompts, you continue to say this word when you are triggered.

As you say your cue word, you may feel sensations in certain parts of your body. As you repeat your word, the feeling or sensation, and the intensity of those feelings may reduce or move. You will want to say the word until the feeling dissipates and you find yourself coming back to your center. The time and repetition of saying your cue word should reduce with time and by utilizing it. You will always acknowledge the trauma, but the goal is to not let it overtake you, and to help you realize that the trauma *isn't happening now*. When I am able to catch myself and say my cue word before I feel debilitated by emotions, my suffering is much shorter and less intense.

Another technique that involves changing neuropathways that I have utilized is Eye Movement Desensitization and Reprocessing (EMDR). I have used this process with two of my therapists. It simply starts with sitting in front of a light bar while the lights move back and forth horizontally. This technique makes a very emotionally and psychologically terrifying experience less powerful. I process a memory as I follow the light with my eyes, and it reprograms the memory to be less disturbing for me. It is amazing to me how it works, but it does. It reduces the hold a memory has on me by changing the neuropathways in my brain that are connected to the memory. This helps me gain more control of the reigns.

I have also been privileged to have experience in art and movement therapy, which id discussed in an earlier chapter. I have been so transformed by those techniques and experiences that I have a long-standing dream to become an art therapist myself. I have dreamed of being a trauma yoga teacher as well. Hopefully, I will achieve both of those dreams. I have been blessed with a long life despite the odds. I've learned that there's always time to transform, to grow, and to go after our dreams.

In addition to the techniques mentioned here, there are so many more for you to try, and I encourage you to discover what works for you. Remember to give yourself grace as you maneuver through the hiccups that will inevitably come up on your path, and to ask for help if you need it. There is no need to sit alone and marinate in your trauma. Healing is an up and down, back and forth process, but there is help out there if you want to reach out and try.

> Life is messy, and so is healing, but you can do it!
> You are proof that you can survive anything!

USING YOUR SENSES

Using your five senses to ground yourself in the present can be another layer of help when you find yourself floating, distracted, and in a general state of imbalance. The five senses are touch, sound, sight, smell, and taste.

My therapist taught me two great ways to work with my senses when I need to bring myself back to the here and now. One way is to go in any order of the senses that I want, and count down what I find. For example, I look for five things to touch or imagine the texture of, like the chair I'm sitting on, and the texture of the pillow next to me. Next, I focus on four things that I hear, from birds chirping to the printer going. Then, I focus on three things that I smell, like the soapy smell or lotion on my skin, two things that I see like the color of the walls, and one thing I can taste or imagine the taste of like chocolate cake. Everything that I point out for the exercise is something I see or connect with in the room I'm in. It's an exercise in investigation and it allows me to discover my place in the environment I find yourself in.

If this seems like too much to keep track of, you can pick any number - like five - and find that many items that fit in each of the five categories. Either way is perfect. The most important thing is to connect with your environment and realize where you fit in it in the present moment. This technique has the potential to fully bring you back from wherever you have dissociated to.

MORE TIPS FOR GROUNDING

Grounding is a very important technique to try to master. If you find yourself dissociating often because of certain stimuli or triggers, focusing on grounding yourself in the present moment is imperative. Mindfulness can be scary, and living with your present situation while trying to heal from your past traumas can be terrifying, but creating a new normal where you live in the now is so fulfilling.

I will outlined several techniques that have worked for me on a daily basis. There are many more ideas that you can try, and techniques that you can explore on your own. You may find that those ideas may work the same or better for you than what I use, but hopefully, these will give you more arrows for your quiver of healing.

Performing mindful breathing-

One of the many ways to do mindful breath work that always works to bring me back to my present self is to inhale for the count of two while bringing my tongue up to the roof of my mouth, and then releasing my tongue down while exhaling for the count of four. As I inhale, I focus on bringing in positivity, and as I exhale, I focus on expelling the negativity from the trauma that has activated me. Doing this exercise in mindfulness is almost like massaging my nervous system, and is a very effective way of grounding.

If you find that your mind is wandering while you breath, it's okay. Use the sound and feel of your breath as your anchoring point, and without judging yourself, refocus on your tongue engaging and releasing from the roof of your mouth. You can do this!

Pushing your heels into the ground-

Feeling your heels burrow in to the floor, or having someone gently step on your toes or on the arches of your feet can also bring you back to the present moment. The gentle pressure brings your consciousness to the floor. It can pull you back down if you are floating above yourself - dissociating because of the situation you are in or the flashback you are dealing with. This pulls yourself down into the earth where so that you can think clearly and then move forward with the next steps to continue to grounding yourself.

Putting ice cubes in your hands-

Holding onto ice cubes and squeezing them in your palms is an excellent way of grounding yourself to the present. The extreme cold brings your consciousness to your hands, the wet drip of the cubes onto the floor creates a feeling and a sound, and the actual sound of you squeezing brings your senses closer to what is happening now. It brings you back to your current situation so that you can think clearer and continue moving forward with your day.

Placing a rubber band around your wrist-

Snapping a rubber band around your wrist whips you into the present moment with the sound of the rubber band expanding and contracting, and the slight sting on your wrist. Please don't use this technique as a punishment. If you feel gratification from the actual sting, please don't do this technique. The sting is just supposed to be a reminder of the here and now, not a symbol or excuse for self-abuse. If you are able to use the rubber band as a tool to catapult you into the present moment, it can be an easy one to ground you.

Using a stress ball-

Using a stress ball as a tool for grounding is an easy way to bring yourself to the present moment. I have a stress ball that I have put essential oil on so that I have two senses working as I squeeze it. I can feel the ball expand and contract under my command, and I can smell the oil getting stronger as I squeeze it. The oil also leaves a scent on my hand. This not only activates the strongest of our senses, but it reminds me of the exercise I just did in the present moment. Even without the oil, this exercise works.

Use your creativity. There are so many ways to help ground yourself. I'm sure you will come up with more!

Music

I have used the power of music in many ways. Classical music resonates with me, and I have used some slower, gentler classical music as a positive trigger that reminds me to slow down. I've used this tool quite often while writing this book and my last three books. This allows me to try to keep my nervous system on a more even keel while I trudge through the difficult memories and issues I have written about.

Classical music may not resonate with you, but you can explore and learn what does. You might even find that you need different types of music to pull you in the direction you need in order to attain balance in different scenarios. For example, if my mind is racing, and the beta waves in my brain are on overdrive to the point of almost reaching a full panic fight or flight stage, I put on intense music (usually rap) and blast it at a level that matches my vibration. Then, I slowly turn the music down and match my vibration to the changes in volume and intensity until I can breathe and think normally again.

I have also utilized the healing power of sound waves by listening to specific frequencies. One of my therapists told me about hertz (Hz) music, and started me off with listening to 432 Hz. I was able to find it on YouTube, and listen to healing and relaxing vibrations when I was ready to go to sleep. I also listened during the day when I needed a reset. There are many choices of Hz frequencies that can help you with a variety of issues, from freeing you from fear, to cleansing your home of negativity. Hertz music has been a very powerful tool for me.

I have also made a soundtrack that I use when I am doing well and want to reinforce being positive about myself. I've made another soundtrack that I listen to when I am having a hard time and need to cry, or emote in some way to release the overwhelming feelings that come up. I've used both soundtracks a lot, and they have helped me gain centeredness.

The art of music is so powerful!

LAND OF SILENT NOTES

Clatter
Every voice in the restaurant
Ranting,
Clanging,
Insistent.

Every conversation
An exclamation.
The cries are crystal clear.

Fight or flight?
There's no escape either way.
Just be
BE!

FEEL it.
Feel IT.

The noise
The repetition
The waves beating against my shore,
Pulling out the sand,
The earth,
The growth.

In HALE
IN hale.

I try to quiet the noise,

The chatter,
The pulse,
The vibrations shattering glass.

Not to silence though...
There is no such thing as silence,
At least not how people think of it.
Stillness Holding your breath
There's no such thing.
There's always a ripple in the sheen.
Even glass is a mirror
    and mirror   glass.

Reactions occur in the silence.
A rest note is a note.
The inhale,
The preparation,
The catalyst,
The what?

Exhale
EXHALE!

SHHHHHhhhhhhh

Silence has sound.
At a different level for me,
For us,
For a cat,
A dog,
A doe.

Maybe we can all just bring it to a hum.

Calming Exercises for Your Nervous System

Many of the calming exercises that I do come from Resources for Resilience by the Association for Comprehensive Energy Psychology (ACEP). They can be found on the organization's website at: https://r4r.energypsych.org/resolving-traumatic-reactions . The site does an excellent job of showing the exercises in picture and video form, and I wanted to introduce you to a couple of them.

Butterfly tapping is a favorite of mine. You simply cross your arms in front of you with your hands resting on the opposite shoulder, and then you alternate tapping the front of your shoulders with each of your hands. It is a gentle reminder to your nervous system to calmly match the rhythm of the tapping. It also uses touch to bring you back to a calmer present moment. When I do it, I tend to tap faster at first to more closely match where my nervous system is, and then control the relaxation or stress and anxiety release by slowly slowing down my tapping to a place I want to be, similar to how I use music as a coping technique.

You can also do a simpler version of this exercise by crossing your arms in front of you with your hands near your shoulders, and pulling down your arm to your elbow. There's an even simpler way to do it if you're in an environment where you don't want to attract any attention by crossing your arms in front of you, holding the position for about a minute, and then switch which arm is in front. Repeat these exercises as many times as you would like.

Another exercise that is helpful to balance me out if I'm in a state of confusion is by tapping the back of my hand. To do this exercise, first make a loose fist with your left hand, take your right fingers and tap the top of your left fist in between the pinky and ring finger. You may find yourself coming back to the present moment quite quickly.

Finally, I want to share an excellent exercise to use when you are in the middle of a trauma response triggered by a memory or flashback. This is a simple one where you do little karate chops on a table or flat surface. All you need to do is gently hit the outside spine of your hand on the flat surface over and over. It has reduced my crippling anxiety and trauma responses for me.

There is also a more in-depth tapping exercise that involves tapping different acupressure points. You can find this one the website, and it is excellent. The video shows it very clearly.

I hope these exercises and the R4R website will be helpful for you!

BREATHE IN

To breathe slowly and evenly
Seemed heavenly.

Dare I try?

With a halting inhale and a rugged exhale
I got scared
Scared of the dry heat swirling in my throat.

It was frightening to feel
This breath and it's rhythmless necessity for life.

To feel me.
Crackly   Strained   Ragged.

I began to imagine myself at the side of a babbling brook.
The water giggling and sighing
Against the rocks and the soil beneath.

My feet tickled by the fish swimming by.
The light of the sun reflecting back on me.
The edges of my dress cold from the fresh water licking it.

I tried to accept breath again in this state.

Intention   Intentional   Intentionality

My inhale became smoother,
My exhale silkier.

I began to feel,
To really FEEL.

Draw in light
Exhale depression

Breathe in peace
Exhale stress

Draw in healing
Exhale sickness

Breathe in peace of mind
Exhale fear

Draw in present moment happiness.

Breathing

Breathing is something most of us rarely think about, and many of us take it for granted because of that. It is a part of our autonomic nervous system, which controls involuntary or unconscious processes like heart rate, digestion, and blood pressure. We don't think about controlling our blood pressure without medication, or speeding up our digestion by focusing on it, but breath is something we can voluntarily manipulate to calm us down, to decrease the effects of stress and trauma, to slow our heart rate and blood pressure, and to center ourselves as we connect to something bigger than ourselves.

Because trauma responses can pull a person in so many directions - from dissociation to panic - using our breath as a tool to bring us back to our center is such an important mechanism to utilize. By being mindful with your breath, you can bring yourself back to the present moment whether you are stuck in the past or are anxiously future-tripping. Practicing these techniques can do wonders to soothe your nervous system.

Using visualization while you concentrate on your breath can be an amazing way to create change inside of you. Even the action of breathing in positivity, and expelling pain and negativity as you exhale, is a powerful discipline to master. It can truly change the trajectory of your day.

For the following examples of mindful breathing, remember to try to expand your breath from your chest to your belly, from your front body and your back body, and from side to side. Allow your breath to swim inside of you and allow it to do its job to help you gain a sense of centeredness. Also, when you exhale you can leave your lips gently closed, or you can sigh out your mouth with your lips gently open to release some of your heat as well.

There are many ways we can control our breath to our benefit and to assist us in positive ways. Here are a few of the simple but powerful ways that I have used:

Making a square -

Breathing by creating a square in your mind's eye is a great way to involve your extra energy and distracted thoughts in an activity while you work to connect to your breath and yourself. Begin by inhaling through your nose for the count of four as you imagine a line going up, sighing out your mouth while making a line to the right, inhaling through your nose for four counts while drawing the line going down, and then exhaling sigh out the mouth to close your square. Another way to make your square is to inhale for four, hold for four, exhale for four and hold for four. Either way is helpful. Experiment to see what is more comfortable for you.

Each time you do it, try to pull out the breathes and make them longer and fuller, expanding your chest front to back and side to side so that you get the full impact of your breath.

Exhaling longer than inhaling –

This technique is effective if you are dissociating and leaving your body as a response to trauma or a trauma memory. First you will inhale with your tongue pulled to the roof of your mouth for the count of four. Then, you will release your tongue down and begin to gently exhale for the count of six. Keep inhaling and exhaling to this count until you feel yourself back in your body and are able to feel your feet on the ground. After that, you can switch your count to an even four and four. Gently inhale for a count of four and then exhale for a count of four, making sure that your breath is smooth. You may even want to do the previously mentioned square breath exercise from above if that helps you picture your breath and keeps you more in your body.

Inhaling longer than exhaling –

This technique is effective when you are feeling heavy and depressed and need to lift out of it. You will essentially be doing the opposite of the above technique. You will start with inhaling bringing your tongue to the roof of your mouth for count of six, and then exhale, dropping your tongue down to the count of four. You can repeat this until you feel yourself rising out of the puddle of your depression. At that point, you can start to inhale and exhale evenly in for the count of 4 and exhale for the count of 4 with the goal of aligning with your present moment self.

Bee breath –

Utilizing bee breath is a wonderful way of reducing anxiety, stress, and the hold that trauma triggers can have on you. To do it, close your eyes if you can, inhale through your nose with your lips closed and exhale while humming like a bumble bee. You will feel a vibration at the back of your throat, and a light buzz at the roof of your mouth and lips. Try to hum with a soft smooth exhale. If your hum is choppy, try to continue to smooth it down with each exhale. Do this three times, take a three-minute break, and then do it again for two more sets.

There are several ways to do bee breath. Some put their index fingers in their ears, and others put their hands in front of their eyes. I like to just close my eyes and allow the buzzing of the bumble bee encompass all of me including my ears. I practice my bee breath twice a day, and I perform it when I get activated by my trauma in between.

Alternate nose breathing –

Alternate nose breathing can be another very effective way to reduce stress and anxiety. To do this the way I learned it in yoga class, you will set your fingers on either side of your nose. First, push your right nostril closed with your right thumb and gently inhale to the count of four. Then release that nostril and close the left nostril with your right ring finger and exhale your breathe out slowly to the count of four. Keep your fingers where they are, and inhale through your right nostril, release your left nostril and put your thumb back on your right nostril again and exhale to the count of four. Do this process for one minute if you can. You can build this practice up to five minutes on each side. Remember, DO NOT force anything. If you feel dizzy or "off" in any way, please stop. This type of breathwork may not be right for you right now. If you are practicing it in a yoga class and don't feel "right" when you are performing it, tell the instructor right away.

With all of these breath practices, always listen to yourself and your body. Don't force anything. Not every practice is for you right now. The most important thing is that you are moving away from the place your trauma takes you, and hugging yourself in to your present moment self. Breath can help tremendously, but so can so many other things such as art, writing, and exercise. Your breath practice will come in time.

Present Moment

Every morning I watch for the animals that cross my path.
I watch with an open heart to see
What they have to tell me about my day.

A hawk – the hunter, adventure, strength.
A woodchuck – trickster, protection for those who believe.
A cat – a visitor from the other side
warning to be watchful and ask for guidance.

Today I saw a hummingbird – fleeting,
present moment happiness.
She fluttered with intention.
Brown, with flashes of red,
her wings a powerful tiny motor.
Vibrated so fast she hovered, floating,
from lantana to butterfly bush, to red fireworks.

Magical, otherworldly,
She left me entranced for the seconds I saw her
It was a gift to be witness to her journey this morning.
I needed her message to live in present moment.
I carried her gift with me all day today.

Present and observant of myself, my surroundings,
My thoughts,
emotions.
As I drove, I read each street sign I passes –
    Riverbend,

Lincoln,
*   Stratford.*
As I cleaned the dishes in my silver metal sink,
I watched the bubbles rise and disappear.
I watered the flowers and paid close attention
to the ones she had graced this morning.
She inspired my gate of breath
The adventure of my day from the outside mundane
Within a meditation.

Tomorrow is tomorrow.

Today, the hummingbird

Living a Good Life and Loving Yourself

The greatest lessons you can learn in your life are how to love yourself, how to find the lovable in others, and how to live a good life... whatever that means to you. For me, I am happy living in a peaceful home surrounded by my pets, husband, and plants, and furthering my mission to help end familial sex trafficking by teaching others.

Living a good life and loving yourself is your success, and it creates change. It positively impacts those around you, and I believe that positivity creates and empowers more positivity. So, you can make a huge impact in the world just by learning to love yourself and living your life with love and compassion towards yourself and others.

You are enough!
You are worthy!
You are loved and lovable!

Yoga

Yoga is such a powerful system and philosophy of movement. It is truly a mind, body, spirit balance that all of us can benefit from. I learned so much while I was enrolled in a 200-hour yoga teaching program that was geared towards the therapeutic benefits and adaptations of yoga. However, I didn't finish the program at the last minute, because it is so hard for me to finish things. I think that my inability to finish things is partially because I had no expectation to survive past my teenage years; therefore, I have a hard time conceiving of my future even now. I also think it's an unconscious way for me to always make myself into a failure so I have yet another reason to beat myself up. I think everyone does that sometimes or in some area of their lives. I just happen to do it in every part of my life. I still gained so much knowledge from the training though, and I really want to share it with you because I think all of us can benefit from it.

Trauma-informed yoga

Trauma-sensitive yoga is an amazing approach to a yoga practice. Trauma really lives within our bodies and our minds, and trauma-informed yoga is a wonderful perspective to teach from regardless of who is in the studio. Trauma survivors are very often in a state of fight or flight. They may have a hard time feeling sensations in their body due to dissociation, or they may feel too much if they are triggered. Being trauma-informed in your teaching can help by including gentle instruction and inviting the concept of choice so that the student is empowered. For example: "You may feel a gentle stretch in your hamstrings." Or "I invite you to close your eyes during this pose if you are comfortable." Or "Regardless of what we are doing, you can always go into Child's Pose if you need to reconnect during class." And "You may feel a sensation here. Just notice it and breathe through it. This moment will end."

This approach allows people to regain control over their bodies and increase present moment awareness which is beneficial for anyone dealing with PTSD. It is especially important for those dealing with Complex Post Traumatic Stress Disorder (CPTSD) which results from someone being exposed to trauma over a long period of time such as from childhood. Trauma-sensitive yoga can help change the programming of destructive thoughts from childhood, to present moment happiness, and it can change your relationship with yourself.

Becoming more comfortable with your body, and being in your body, is an important goal. According to the yoga instructor David Emerson, "The more comfortable we get having a body that is feel-able and muscle dynamics that are ...under our control, the more we heal the impact of complex trauma."[11] As a teacher and a student of yoga, I have found that I can connect on a deeper level with my students, and in a more intimate way with myself and my energy through trauma-sensitive yoga.

Adaptations

Using yoga blocks, bolsters, or blankets are wonderful, useful, and often needed tools to bring your body into alignment during your yoga practice. They are not just for use if you have an injury. They are imperative tools for use when you need a little extra support, a lift to help you gain alignment with your posture in a pose, or to aid in any other way. Always go into class with a couple of blocks and a small blanket unless you have access to them at the studio you go to. Without these tools you may find yourself struggling through a pose and knocking your mind, body, and spirit into a tailspin of frustration, and feeling incapable of doing what you are capable of doing with a little extra support. Remember that yoga is a practice. It isn't about perfection. It's a practice.

Chair yoga

Chair yoga is a wonderful way to do yoga when you have physical challenges that require more support for your practice. Before you start, you will want a sturdy chair without a soft cushion so that you don't sink into the chair. If you need a boost in order for your feet to be flat, you can lay a blanket flat on the seat. If you need a little lift to help you sit tall, you can also roll a blanket to put under your sit bones which will help your back float right above your hips creating instant good posture. If your feet are floating above the floor, taking a couple of yoga blocks and putting one underneath each foot is a wonderful way to create support for your legs. Performing chair yoga is a wonderful way for anyone to hone their skills and gain the same benefits as a standing practice.

You can adapt an entire class using the chair following the same exercises as a standing practice. For example, you can inhale your arms above your head and exhale bend forward for an uttanasana (standing forward fold). You can do a tree pose by standing perpendicular to the chair, hold onto the back of the chair with your right hand, have your left arm out to the side so it matches in height to the right, and put your right foot onto the seat of the chair. This mimics the standing unsupported tree pose, and it has the same benefits of strengthening your core, and improving your balance. One more example is the balasana pose (child's pose). You can stand in front of the seat of your chair, bend your knees gently, inhale your arms up and exhale them to the back of the seat. If you have more movement in your body, you can even fold over more, and exhale your arms to the seat of the chair.

Poses that are great for reducing anxiety and stress:

There are many poses that can soothe your nervous system, but I want to highlight six poses that you can explore...

<u>Standing with hands at heart center</u> seems like an overly simple way to reduce stress and anxiety, but it's very beneficial. Standing or sitting with your palms together in a prayer position right in front of your sternum and allowing yourself to close your eyes and breathe gently and evenly can be the exact thing you need to center yourself and reduce your anxiety level.

<u>Child's pose</u> is another relieving pose where you bring yourself to the floor or mat, kneel, and exhale your torso to the floor with your arms outstretch in front of you on the mat. Keep inhaling and exhaling deeply, allowing yourself to reach further forward with every exhale while allowing your sternum to reach for the mat. When I do child's

pose, I imagine my stress and feelings of pain drip out of my sternum and into the ground. The earth can take it, I promise. Child's pose is also a restorative pose, which I talk about a bit later in the chapter.

Extended puppy pose starts with you on your hands and knees in a tabletop position. Next, you walk your hands forward while allowing your sternum to reach for the mat. You support yourself by having your forearms reach the mat in front of you. Much like the child's pose, you will breathe deeply and continue to reach and sink in the mat.

Downward facing dog pose starts with you on hands and knees in a tabletop position. Next, lift your tailbone towards the sky and elongate the spine while gently pulling your shoulder tips towards your hips which further extends and elongates your spine and torso. Don't forget to breathe!

Eagle pose is an excellent pose to reduce stress and anxiety by crossing your left and right hemisphere. First stand with your feet hips width apart in mountain pose, gently bend your knees, wrap your right leg over your left leg or ankle (whichever you have available for you), and then wrap your right arm under your left elbow reaching your palms together and up towards the sky. If crossing your arms isn't available for you, you can bring your hands and forearms together in a prayer position with your elbows parallel to your sternum. Slowing your breath in this pose allows both sides of your body and mind to relax and release in an amazing way while improving and extending your balance inside and out.

Inversions are excellent for the blood flow and the lymphatic system. They are also great for reducing stress and anxiety as well as releasing trauma in the body. The legs-up-the-wall pose is an excellent gentle inversion that is available for most of us, where you lay on your back on the floor and bring your legs up onto the wall as close to 90 degrees as is available to you. Then, you breathe deeply. I have explained how you can support yourself further in this pose in the "restorative yoga" section of this chapter.

Restorative yoga

Restorative yoga is away to perform yoga positions on the floor that are fully supported with bolsters, blankets, and the floor. It is all about release, being uplifted, and relaxation. I want to include a few examples that you can incorporate into your day. I have gained a huge benefit from using supported restorative yoga because I can sink into the pose, stay there for a few minutes while my body and mind get on the same page, and then gently go to the next pose.

One wonderfully therapeutic pose is supported child's pose. For this pose, you want to kneel and then sit on both of your feet. If your feet are sensitive, you can lay a blanket under the tops of your feet. Next, you want to lay a bolster on the floor in the same direction as your torso, inhale, and then exhale your body forward onto the bolster. Your arms will bend to your sides with your hands on either side of the bolster. Gently turn your head to the right or the left so you can breathe easily. If you find that the back of your knees become uncomfortable, you can place a blanket behind them for further support.

As you can see, the amount of support is endless. You add and subtract blankets, bolsters, towels, and washcloths... whatever makes your practice the most comfortable and the most uplifted.

Another restorative pose is viparita karani (legs-up-the-wall-pose) where you place a very low bolster or blanket against the wall, place your low back on the blanket and your legs up the wall. You can relax your feet, and relax your arms out to the side and breathe. Allow your body and your mind to relax in this gentle inversion.

Yin yoga

Yin yoga is all about sustained stillness. In this practice, you will hold a pose for minutes and allow your body and mind to sink into to the pose in order relax the mind and to stretch the fascia, or connective tissue, that we all have in our bodies.[13] Fascia is an amazing part of our bodies. It connects to every organ, muscle, nerve, artery, and vessel inside of the body. Holding yin yoga poses for long periods of time is the only way for fascia to respond and release, creating a more supple body and spirit. It is important to know how long to hold each pose, so having a good teacher is important. Over stretching is just as dangerous as not stretching at all.

In terms of the mind aspect of yin yoga, your thoughts may have a fit while you are staying still. That is normal. What is important is to listen to your racing thoughts and remind them that it's okay. That you're safe. That this moment will end and another will begin. With your mind and body both working on extending themselves, and on extending discipline and patience, you can gain a new level of peace.

I have also learned so much about my inner strength and energy from yoga. I learned that I am powerful, and that my energy can both support and receive from others. Your energy extends past you and can touch the energy of another person in class for example. No need to tactically touch, just know that you are not only connecting to yourself and to spirit, but that you are connecting to other people through a bubble of energy of your creation that is surrounding you.

Hopefully this will inspire you to find a local studio to practice and gain more knowledge! Just remember to allow these movements, poses, and shapes serve you not only where you are in your body, mind and spirit now, but where you want to go. Try to always extend your practice with the intent of curiousity, not with force and unreasonable expectation.

You can do it, and you deserve it!

Meditation

Using meditation as a life skill will help you not only with your relationship to your trauma, but I've also found that it has helped me with general anxiety and depression. Setting an intention at the start of your meditation, and letting it swirl in your mind, body and spirit, can create a balance that can be soothing for your nervous system. The stillness of sitting or lying down to meditate can be difficult for someone on the healing path from trauma, so moving meditation can be beneficial to start with.

Performing a seated or lying meditation on a mat or specific space, can bring your energy to that space, and every time you go back to it that energy is there to greet you. Start with an intention you want to mediate on, and then begin your journey.

If you decide to do a seated meditation, feel your seat on the floor or mat. Also, feel your sit bones and where your lower back, shoulders and head are in alignment with your base. Next, feel your knees and their relationship with the mat, where your feet are touching the mat, and then start intentional breathing. Allow your breath to fill your body front to back and side to side. Allow your head to sit softly on your neck, let your neck relax, your arms and hands relax, and move all the way down your body. Then, release your concentration on your breath and focus on your center, your energy swirling, and the intention you started your meditation with.

With years of practice and giving myself grace, I have achieved a meditation practice where I lay on the floor, cultivate my breath in through my nose and out through my mouth, feel the breath enter into every cell of my body, and then release control of my breath and allow it to serve me in the relaxed state I have created. Then, I allow any negativity I'm holding onto to pour out of my back and into the floor, through the basement, and into the earth where I know nature can absorb it. As I am letting go of past traumas and pain, I focus on healing energy and light swirling around me, my entire body, my third eye (a spot on your forehead between your eyes), and my inner spirit. When I combine this movement of negativity and positivity, I feel more alive, more centered, and more ready to move forward in my day and my life. It can be a very powerful practice.

Moving meditation can be as simple as walking or doing the dishes. I practice moving mediation throughout the day to try to bring intention into my day. In walking meditation, for example, you want to feel your heel touch the floor and then the ball of the foot, and then your toes. If you slow it down enough, you can even put one toe down at a time. You feel the muscles in your calves and thighs propel you forward to the next step, you focus on how your arms are moving opposite to your steps, and where your head is facing as you go from room to room. When I do the dishes, I focus on the temperature of the water, and I allow any negativity I have stored up to drip off my hands and down the drain with the soapy water I'm cleaning with. It is truly an exercise in intention, and it can be very healing and soothing to your nervous system.

Walking outside is another powerful moving meditation exercise. Combining the focus on your heel toe gate with feeling the breeze, smelling the grass, hearing birds chirp, and seeing leaves rustling in the wind, can be very powerful to ground you in present moment.

Whether you are doing a sitting or lying meditation session, or a moving meditation, it's so important to allow your thoughts to travel through you. I haven't found a way to eliminate intrusive thoughts while I am practicing meditation. The important thing to remember is that thoughts will go in and thoughts will go out. Let them pass through without focusing on them and then come back to your breath or movement.

And always remember to give yourself grace!

YOGA NIDRA

I wanted to give you an example of a type of meditation called yoga nidra that I created for myself and my loved ones. Yoga nidra is an amazing practice that allows you to rest and release deeply, and it can facilitate healing. It is a type of guided meditation that will allow you to connect and let go at the same time, and can allow healing to occur in both your body and your mind. When you allow yourself to release into it, you can feel a sensation of weightlessness like you are floating in water. The practice of yoga nidra, with repetition, can go through five phases of neurological activity from a state of deep relaxation to two simultaneous states of sleep and conscious awareness, and then to the highest level of meditation.[13] It can connect and help you embody the states of acceptance, compassion, and a pure awareness of yourself and your surroundings.

Before you begin, you can ask someone you trust to read this yoga nidra meditation to you and then you can do the same for them. If you want to do it alone, you can record your own voice and play it for yourself. You can move through the meditation seated and focus on your breathing every step of the way. You can also play calming music or vibrations if that helps you get closer to connection.

Hopefully, you will gain a great benefit from practicing yoga nidra. Each time you do a session of twenty to twenty-five minutes, your body and mind have the capability to connect on a deeper level. It has truly helped me with my symptoms of trauma, from extreme anxiety and depression, to dissociation.

There are many examples of this practice that you can try. Hopefully, the one I've created will be a great start for you. I hope you enjoy it!

First, find a safe place to allow yourself to relax and connect with yourself. Next, find a comfortable recline with pillows and blankets to support you. You could lay in bed, on a yoga mat, or on your lawn. Just do what makes sense to you.

As you meditate, your partner will read the commands below in a soft voice, or you'll listen to the recording you made of yourself reading them. While you listen, you can just focus on the person's soft, easy voice, you can have music in the background, you can use Hertz music, or you can just invite a gentle wind to keep you company. Again, it's up to you. Although mindfulness and letting go can be scary because it may feel different at first, remember that every thought and movement will come and go – start and stop. Make this process about and for YOU.

- *After you've found a comfortable reclined position, feel the fabric, mattress or ground beneath your upper back, your lower back, your hips and your lower body.*

- *Feel the pillow that is supporting your neck and head. Is it soft? Is it sturdy? Is your back supported and comfortable? How about your feet?*

- *Once you've found a comfortable place and space to sink in, let yourself begin to release, and allow your eyes to gently close if you feel comfortable.*

- *If you fall asleep that is fine. Your mind's eye is hearing my voice and connecting.*

- *Take in a nice deep breath in through your nose and let your tongue touch the roof of your mouth. Exhale sigh out your breath.*

- *Inhale deeply in through your nose let your breath fill your ribs up and down, side to side, feel your back body extending, exhale sigh out your mouth.*

- *Now take a third deep breath, and focus on your exhale pulling all the way down to your lower belly*

- *Inhale nice and deep, exhale let the energy of your breath go all the way down to your hips and thighs.*

- *The last inhale you will focus on, breathe deeply in through your nose and exhale fully down to your toes.*

- *Now you can release control of your breath, let it gently circle, and know you are connected from head to toe.*
- *Let that breath focus up your front with ease, let your breath do what it already knows how to do.*
- *Bring your focus to your toes from your right pinky toe all the way to your big toe, now your left pinky toe, all the way to the big toe.*
- *Now bring your mind's eye to the arch of your foot, and let your consciousness drip down underneath to the heel of your foot.*
- *Is your heel touching the floor? Is it the side or the center of your heel that is touching?*
- *Now over to the left foot, feel the arch, top and bottom, and down to your heel.*
- *Keep relaxing with your breath and then bring your mind to your right ankle, feeling the rt side where your bone protrudes, and then allow it to circle over to the left side.*
- *Now allow your mind's eye to feel the rt side of the calf, your shin, and down to the left side of the calf.*
- *Notice if there is any tension. If there is any, just release it with your next exhale, and remember you are completely supported by your mat, the floor, or the mattress you are laying on.*
- *Do the same with your left leg, circling your ankle, and gently focusing on your left calf, shin, and belly of the calf.*
- *Now notice if there's any tension in the left leg, and if it feels different than the right in any way.*
- *Next bring your focus to your right knee, circle the top to the bottom, and then allow yourself to focus on your thigh. The top of the thigh to the inside of the thigh and then the underside of the thigh to the outside. Allow your consciousness to envelope your entire knee and thigh, and feel where your hamstring is touching your mat.*

- *As you circle back to the top of your right thigh, start to journey to the top of your left knee, drip down to the side of knee, then the bottom of the knee.*
- *Next pull your energy up the left quadricep, surrounding it with your energy, and then pull it down to the hamstring.*
- *Feel where your left hamstring is touching the ground, mattress, or mat and if there is any tightness let it release down through the mat, through the floor, and down into the earth below.*
- *Remember that Nature can take all of your discomfort for you. It's okay to release.*
- *Also allow yourself to notice areas that are loose and supple. Deeply inhale and exhale.*
- *Allow your breath to wash up the front of your body and wash down your back, knowing that you are connected to yourself and the universe.*
- *Now let your mind's eye travel to the front of your right hip flexor the right side of your hip to the right buttock, swing across your sacrum to your left buttock, left side of hip, and left hip flexor.*
- *Now to your lower belly, your middle belly, your solar plexus, which is the connection to your sternum.*
- *Wash across your right ribs to your back, lower back, middle back, connecting to the spine.*
- *Wash down the thoracic spine to the lumbar, the left lower back, the left middle back, slide around your ribcage to the front, connecting to the sternum.*
- *And breathe ... inhale and exhale at your own pace, feel your ribcage expanding and contracting.*
- *Your body knows what to do. There's no need to try to control or restrict it.*
- *Just be...*

- *Just notice here in this moment how your feel.*
- *Are you expanding your energy? There's no limit give yourself permission to release what you don't need or want and give yourself permission to attain what you want.*
- *Now continue on to the front of your right chest, slide up to your shoulder, feel the ball and socket easily engaged, relax the muscles down your bicep and tricep to your elbow, front of the forearm, back of the forearm, your wrist, thumb, first finger, middle finger, ring finger, and baby finger.*
- *Feel your energy extend beyond your hands.*
- *Tiptoe back up the arm to the shoulder, slide across the chest to the left side. Feel your ribcage on this side, and feel our chest rise and fall with ease, go to your left shoulder, feel that socket, the ball is balanced in the socket, you are balanced, down the bicep, the tricep, the elbow, front of forearm, back of forearm, wrist, thumb, first finger, middle finger, ring finger, and pinky finger.*
- *Feel the energy extend down past your left fingers.*
- *Tiptoe up your left arm all the way up to the shoulder.*
- *Slide across the clavicle from the left to the right.*
- *Bring your mind's eye to the back-body. The scapula, the top the ribs, the upper thoracic and cervical spine. Walk all the way up the seven cervical vertebrae to the base of your skull. Bring yourself down the left side to the left scapula, the left back body, upper ribs, upper thoracic and walk back up the left side of cervical spine to base of the skull.*
- *Notice if there's any tension here. It's easy to get tension in your upper back, shoulders and neck, but it's also easy to release if you give yourself permission.*
- *Try to do that now.*
- *Let your energy move to the front of your face, your right jawline, the tip of your chin, the dimple underneath your lips,*

your right lower lip, your right upper lip, your left lower lip, your left upper lip, the dimple above your lips, the tip of your nose, right nostril, left nostril, right nose above the nostril, and the left nose above the nostril.

- *Go across the bridge of the nose to the right cheek bone, the left cheek bone, underneath the right eye, your eyelid, your eyebrow, underneath your left eye, your eyelid, your left eyebrow.*

- *Now go to the space between your eyebrows, then slightly above to the third eye, left forehead, right forehead.*

- *Slide down to the right earlobe, the right eardrum, the right top of the ear, left earlobe, left eardrum, the top of the left ear.*

- *Now go to the middle of your hairline to the crown of your head.*

- *Feel white light swirling, protecting you around the crown of your head, creating a space for you to elevate and for you to connect with ourself and the universe.*

- *Feel that white light washing over you gently but powerfully.*

- *Feel that connection to yourself, to your place in this universe, to this present moment, this moment in time.*

- *Feel a connection to your past and a connection to your future. Feel protected, feel whole, feel loved.*

- *Let this love from yourself to yourself - from the universe to the universe - and let it wash down your body now going head to toe front to back smoothly, in a perfect temperature whatever that is for you. Let it gently wash over you.*

- *You decide... does it feel like honey? Or does It feel like river water? Either way, let it drip all the way down the body, your forehead, your shoulders, our arms, your belly, your hips, thighs, knees, shins, all the way down to your toes.*

- *Feel your breath as being smooth, and enriching*

- *Feel the comfort of this moment.*
- *Now start to bring yourself back.*
- *Take all of the strength and love with you and start to wriggle your toes and fingers gently, slowly bring your knees up so your feet are flat on the ground and gently allow your knees to fall side to side waving to the sky or the ceiling above.*
- *Now allow your body to fall all the way to the right. Curl your knees in a little bit. Let your left arm rest in front of your heart. Your right arm can become your pillow.*
- *Start to feel where your side-body is touching the ground. When you are ready use the strength of your left arm to push yourself up to a comfortable seat.*
- *With hands at heart center, you can slowly blink your eyes open now.*
- *Know you are still surrounded by that white light coming from within and coming from all of the good that's around you.*
- *Take one more nice deep breath. Inhale and then exhale sigh out the mouth.*
- *Feel the connection of your sacrum to the earth.*
- *From my heart to yours,*

-Namaste

Self-Care is a Beautiful Thing

Allowing yourself to care about yourself is imperative for healing. What I didn't realize is that there is more to it than just allowing yourself to take a day off, or sink into a warm bubble bath. I learned a wonderful way of thinking about self-care from one of my therapists. She said that there are three types of self-care, and that it is very important to try to include all three and to include them in balance. The three types are productivity, joy, and rest or relaxation.

I have found that I am very good at productivity. I make lists and then lists of lists to organize my day so that I have a framework of activity. I want to keep myself going in a certain direction, and I feel like it is easier to stay in the present moment when I'm productive. Writing this book, doing laundry, going to all of my many doctor appointments, and feeding and taking care of my fur babies all fall under productivity, and they are definitely part of caring for myself. Writing gives me an amazing outlet, doing things around the house makes my environment more peaceful, and I am taking care of myself by going to my check-ups and therapy appointments. Taking care of my fur babies falls under all three types of self-care – my pets bring me so much joy and they help me through so much of what I go through every day!

Joy is the second wing of self-care, and I have a hard time with it. I have a hard time with identifying the things that actually give me joy, and then making time for them. I know it seems like it should be easy, but when I ask myself what brings me joy, I get stumped after saying my husband, my cats, and my friends. My therapist reminded me that artwork gives me joy, so I have added that. Then I was given homework to think of more. After a lot of contemplation, I included being in nature, taking photographs, cooking, and watching football. Again, I know that I love all of those things, but for some reason, naming them as things that bring me joy and are a part of my self-care was difficult for me. It also made me realize that I am not giving enough time and energy to the joys in my life.

Rest and relaxation are an even harder type of self-care for me. I have a very hard time finding ways to unwind. Other than watching television, I am horrible at pampering myself, or taking naps if my body is asking for it. I actually feel guilty. I know that I'm not alone in this, but it is so important for us to take care of ourselves in this way. Our bodies and minds need a break from the stresses and pressures of life. We deserve and need to rest.

Giving to others is another type of self-care. I know that I feel amazing when I help someone else. My husband and I go around the city of Detroit at least a couple of times a year and distribute clothes that we want to give away to homeless people. It is so rewarding to stop the car, ask if a person needs a coat, a shirt, or a pair of shoes and give them what they need right there. I remember giving a yellow shawl to a woman, and when we swung around about an hour later to go home, we saw her spinning in circles with her shawl outstretched waving in the wind she was creating. It was so touching. I am tearing up right now as I think of the joy on her face.

Caring for yourself on these levels truly is a gift. I'm trying to balance myself by utilizing all three pillars of self-care as equally as possible. I am definitely a work in progress, but just realizing that there is so much to self-care has helped me tremendously. I hope it helps you too!

Water

Taking a bath or shower can be a powerful way to allow yourself to heal physically, mentally, and emotionally. The warmth and the amazing healing properties of water provide amazing opportunities for you to move forward through some difficult body memories, and uplift you as you process your feelings.

To immerse yourself in bath water - the buoyancy and the sound of silence in the water - can be immensely soothing for some people.

For those that aren't able to take a bath for whatever reasons, a shower can be just what you need. I am in the shower camp. Showering is an amazing opportunity to focus your breath, to slow down your nervous system, to listen to the water hitting your body and the floor and to succumb to its intensity. A wonderful exercise you can use to rid yourself of some negativity is to focus on a negative feeling, like "I am ugly", mentally turn it into honey, and then watch it wash down your body with the water. Focus on it going down the drain away from you never to return again. You can also do this with larger thoughts like "I am a burden", or you can simply focus on the stress of the day washing down the drain. Whatever you need to do is the right choice, and it will make you feel lighter and more ready to face the day or the night ahead.

You may have trauma related to baths or showers, but hopefully you don't have trauma related to both techniques. Personally, I have a grave fear of taking a bath, and I have tried to make myself do it every couple of years to no avail. My brother almost drowned me when I was seven-years-old. He wanted to see what would happen, and what happened was that I choked, threw up, and inhaled a bunch of water. I almost drowned. I haven't gotten over it yet, or at least my body hasn't. As a result, my body memories of that experience have hijacked me and prevented me from doing the bath exercise. I will keep working on it though. Every couple of years I will try again.

Cooking and Baking

Cooking and baking are both an art and a science. They can be very playful and therapeutic activities. I don't tend to follow any recipe to the "T". instead, I look at it for the basic idea, and then I use my intuition to get the result I would like. I encourage everyone to flex their creative abilities while cooking, and play with their ingredients a bit.

I have found myself falling into my batter with all my good intentions and created peanut butter biscotti from a cookie recipe, and iced lemon nut bread out of a cake recipe. I also cook with a bit of whimsy, creating fajita burritos, or chicken a la Adira.

I also cook with color. I always make sure I have at least three colors in each of my meals. Whether it's steak with red, yellow, or orange bell peppers and green peas, or dirty rice with black beans, peppers, and white rice, I want to consume color. It makes your meal more joyous.

It is so rewarding to create with a bit of flair and be able to feed yourself and your family with a meal crafted from your heart. I love watching my husband take his first bite and see the smile on his face after his first swallow. There's nothing better than nourishing the ones that you love with a meal made from your soul.

Gardening

As long as it isn't a hot and excessively humid day, I love to garden with my bare hands. That way I can search for grounding without any barriers. If it's too humid, it reminds me of being buried at five-years-old, and I avoid going outside all together. But if it's not, gardening is heaven.

I love the feeling of the dirt, its coolness beneath the surface, and its thick heavy texture which I can imagine would make a beautiful pot in a ceramics class. The surface is often grainier like a thick version of sand, inviting moisture wherever it can get it.

Every spring, I create a haven for myself and my husband on our little back deck. I surround us with pots of plants and flowers that range from rose bushes to cacti, from tall grasses to orange lantana flowers, and from sage to spearmint plants. As they grow throughout spring and summer, we are more and more closed in by this secret garden oasis where nobody can see us, and we can grow limp their arms.

I thank goodness for the earth every day. What an amazing heart to fall in love with.

Life Finds a Way

*Through the cracks in the desert sand
hardened by the rain,
Life finds a way
with a sharp and pointy play*

*Through the potholes in the street
where tire parts keep them company,
Life finds a way
in a crushing piled heap*

*Through the breaks in the tide
where the ocean sighs and weeps,
Life finds a way
in a swirling, crashing leap*

*From the depth to the light
to the earth's fresh air,
Life finds a way
to hope,
to faith,
to be.*

Positive Affirmations

Positive affirmations are important expressions that keep your consciousness on the path to growth and healing. There are many ways to utilize this tool. The best way to empower yourself through words is up to you… what do you respond to?

Saying affirmations to yourself can be difficult. It can be hard to break through negative self-talk and images because of what you have been programmed to think of yourself. That is why using the power of your words is so important. You are battling against some steadfast beliefs that simply aren't true, but they are nevertheless ingrained in your consciousness. Using these positive affirmations can interrupt the negativity you are married to, and actually create new and healthy neuropathways in your brain so that you can replace the negative with the positive. These affirmations can help you court happiness instead of hatred. Your perspectives can truly change with a little work.

It is important to write and say your affirmations in the present tense. That way, you are telling yourself that what you've written is true in the present moment, even if you don't quite believe it's true right now. Doing this exercise in the present tense will instruct your subconscious and will get your conscious mind that much closer to believing the statements are true. Here are some examples of some positive affirmations:

- I am a good and blessed person
- I am grateful
- I am proud of myself
- I am strong
- I am a survivor
- I am safe
- I am healing every day

- I am beautiful/handsome inside and out
- I am smart
- I am enough
- I am one with nature
- I am a warrior
- I love myself
- I am loved
- I love my body
- I am valuable
- I am giving
- I am courageous
- I am an important part of the universe
- I am trying

Here are a few ways to write out your affirmations so you can battle against negativity:

Write your truths down on cards –

You can cut little cards out of larger pieces of paper, or use index cards to write your affirmations on. I have painted large pieces of paper and cut out smaller cards to put mine on. This makes the process a little more enjoyable. You can use any form of art to make them, from printmaking, to making them out of cloth. Do whatever feels right to you!

Write your positive affirmations on sticky notes –

You can put your sticky notes on your mirrors, your refrigerator, your microwave, or any other place where you look during the day. It presents a wonderful opportunity to say your affirmations if you have them right in front of you during your daily activities, and it allows you to say them throughout the day.

Say your affirmations like a mantra that you can count on a mala –

I have a mala (a strand of beads to count mantras on) with a 108 count of beads and I say my positive affirmations like a mantra. "I am a good and blessed person" is one bead, then "I am beautiful", and so on. When I reach my last one, I start over. My goal is to add one new affirmation every day. Sometimes I can't think of one, and that's okay. Thankfully, tomorrow is another opportunity to add to my list.

Write your truths in your journal. –

If you journal daily, write your affirmations down in a dedicated space. I would also add any new affirmations you came up with on a particular day to the top of that page's entry so you can see your progress in two ways – in list form, and as a part of your daily writings.

Write your affirmations in your planner –

Writing messages to yourself in your daily planner can really make an impact throughout your day as you reference your schedule. I have even bought positive affirmation stickers and added them to my calendar so that I have either a message or a beautiful Image to draw my eye to each day. I have stickers that say things like, "progress not perfection", "you deserve to rest today", and "love yourself fully". Because of my love of plants, I even have stickers that say "plant lady" with a bunch of beautiful foliage. These stickers just make me happy! Beyond that, adding these reminders has really helped me. My stickers also brighten other people's days when they see the happy stickers while I'm making appointments. I've even handed them out to others to hopefully make their day.

Have fun with your affirmations!
YOU ARE WORTH IT!

Also keep in mind that affirmations aren't just for adults. They are important for children to say and practice affirming themselves as well. What better way is there to encourage a positive self-worth than for children to reinforce it in themselves at a young age? Just like you would teach safety tactics, have rules for going to bed on time, and closely monitor their screen time and internet use, encouraging affirmations is a tool that will be useful throughout their life. Affirmations will help them gently fortify the strength of their inner world.

So, let's encourage positivity in our youth as well through affirmations as well!

AFFIRMATIONS 2

SHAME

Shame is such a tricky sticky word,

riddled with conflict.

Riddled with sadness,

anger,

and twisted disgrace.

    Recently, I was going through the pictures I had taken of houses I remembered being abused in. Then, I looked up associated names for the properties by searching through the Wayne County Register of Deeds website. I also did the reverse, and looked up houses associated with people that I know abused me. After doing both of these actions, I had hit a wall in my research skills, and was unable to look into them further.

    One of my friends is an expert researcher; together we looked at one the many houses owned by my pediatrician, and I recognized it! It was so surreal to see this house and know that I had been abused in it. It was in Wayne County, but it was farther away from the cluster of houses I had information on. I wonder if my parents drugged me before I went to it, or if it was one of the places I was forced to lay on the floorboards of the car until I got there. Maybe it was one of the times I was chloroformed before going there. I don't know for sure, but as soon as I saw a picture of it on Google Maps, my eyes got wide and I just knew it. I had been there, and terrible things had happened to me there.

    Right after that, we looked into one of the homeowners of another house I remembered being raped in. After looking in her database and Newspapers.com we found him. We found his picture on a newspaper article that talked about what an upstanding person he was in the community. Once again, when I saw his picture, my eyes got wide. This time, tears began to brim in my eyes, and I was left in a state of shock. I pointed at the computer screen, "That's him! That's him!" My friend looked at me with care in her eyes - a witness to my trauma response of shaky hands, tears, and a shade of melanin stripped from my face. I could see my shock mirrored in her eyes. And this was just one perpetrator. What if she could help me find more?

After that initial shock, she was able to find his current address, phone number, and age, and I didn't know what to do. I'd thought I would know what to do if this situation ever arose, but I didn't know what to do. I was so conflicted, and I felt a deep-seated pang of shame as a result. Three weeks later, the pang has morphed into a knife wound.

As I deal with the potential shame of not doing anything with the information I have on my abuser, I am solidifying the feelings of shame from my childhood. The shame that I know really isn't mine in my head - it's my parents' it's my rapists', it's my brother's, it's my uncles'. It's not mine. I couldn't have told anyone. I knew it as soon as I was buried up to my neck in a makeshift grave that I couldn't tell anyone, but I can't seem to stop the feeling that I could've saved lives if I had. I could've saved other kids from my father - from my parents.

And then I'm catapulted back to the present moment. I feel shame that I am even thinking of letting this information stay on a piece of paper rather than taking it to law enforcement. Shame that I'm petrified. Petrified! *But I'm an adult*, I tell myself. *I can take care of myself. I can ask for help if I need it.* But I'm petrified.

Fear is my captor. Even though I know my fear is legitimate, I feel shame because of it. There were so many high-powered people in the ring that abused me, and there is the next generation of people that I can only imagine are powerful as well. It's obvious that not everyone is dead. If they were, I wouldn't be writing this.

I wouldn't be in a state of panic.

I wouldn't be floating above my body watching my fingers type this right now.

Just breathe. I tell myself. *Just inhale and exhale with intention.*

So, I'm breathing while I wait for my higher self to decide what to do. Meanwhile, I have reached out to the FBI again to ask some questions on the statute of limitations and whether they would take on such an old case. Maybe that will help me. Maybe those answers and the possible support from law enforcement will ease my fears. We will see.

I'm trying to remember that either way, I am honoring myself and other survivors by writing my books, by speaking to the public, and by doing other things to help the movement to end familial child sex trafficking. I'm still a warrior either way. I'm still a survivor and a warrior.

I'm just side-stepping in circles right now.

I'm walking in circles, but I'm still walking, and sometimes that's enough.

Sometimes that's enough for all of us.

Untitled

Sadness grows and flourishes here
    inside my heart and soul.
Sometimes I can push it away
    and make sunshine appear.
The sunshine comes not by itself
    but is made with much effort
        from the core of my heart.
The sadness takes on the persona of a vampire
    trying to steal the sunshine inside me.
        trying to rob me of happiness.
It is a constant battle for this light inside
    this light behind a thick cloak of
        ominous black.
I know this light shines bright and sure
    behind this cloak of black.
I know it fights with courage and
    determination to break through the
        barrier.
I'm afraid this battle may be never ending,
    for the vines of despair grow rapidly
        though the sunshine cuts like a
            gallant sword.
I just hope that the strength from within
    will have the courage and determination
        to survive the choking black.
I'm trying with all my might to help the
    sunshine grow stronger.
I hope I can find the courage within to
    never give in and fight.

        -Written by me when I was 16 years old

BLINDS

I look through the blinds people peek at me through.
They try to see me for me, but they don't.
Only I can see all of the holes and
the breaks in the rhythm of their vertical stance.

The blinds click
                clack
                      slap

The outsiders think I'm straight
Even
A solid hue.
A hummed note.
But I see where the blinds are broken and bent.

I try to staple them
Tape them
Bolt them
Glue them
But still there is a harsh gap between each slat

These people want me to be fixed,
So they see what they want.

Click
        click
                Swoosh

Then I Scream!

BEDTIME

Last night I found myself in the middle of a whirlwind of my memories. Not a dream, not a nightmare, but a flashback that I unfortunately have very often. These flashbacks are truly night terrors, and I had both of them in one night.

The flashback started with me running in bed before I went to sleep. My legs started to churn without my instruction, trying to dislodge the trainer that my mother made me sleep with to stretch out my vaginal opening for the clients. It was a nightly ritual that replaced the goodnight kiss my friends got from their mothers. I never could get it out, but I tried to do it in a way where I wasn't breaking any rules. If I took out this painful tool with my hands, I don't know what my punishment would have been, but I didn't want to find out. Kicking my knees up in a movement somewhere between a marching band member and a track runner was the only way I could figure out to expel it. As I whip into a restless sleep, I can only assume that the churning continued because my legs had cramped up by the time I woke up in the middle of the night from the second night terror.

I woke up vomiting and choking from my second flashback. I was throwing up what was left behind from one of the clients. I remember his features so clearly. He had a long face with a harsh angle to his jaw and chin, and his eyes were steely, tipping towards grey even though I knew that they were a light blue. He had dirty blonde hair that was parted on his left and my right. I could tell that normally it was combed just so, but when he came to my bed the front of his hair would wisp down his face. Then, it would silently whip back and forth reaching out to me and then back onto his forehead. His smooth forehead would create beads of sweat in the summer time, and remain dry in the winter. He had a bold mole on his right cheek just below his eye. He was always dressed like he'd just left work, as if I was his five o'clock drink to help him wind down from his day. His only words to me were, "stay still... stay still... That's it... stay still". So I did. After he left, I often ended threw up.

My body remembers both of those experiences so crystal clear, and it is still trying to work through them. All I can do is be a vessel for the running, the abuse, and the throwing up of the evidence. It is a horrible feeling to go through time and time again, but I can't seem to stop it. I know I've survived it and moved on to a safe life, but my body and my subconscious still don't realize it.

So last night I got up, washed myself off, brushed my teeth, and fixed myself a cup of tea with a lot of honey while I continued to cough for about an hour. Going back to sleep on nights like that is not an option, so I pull out my phone and try to tackle sodoku or a puzzle, and invite one of my cats to my bed for company, reassuring him that I will no longer kick and flail.

FBI

I went downtown to talk with two agents at the Federal Bureau of Investigation (FBI) about my story yesterday. I can't believe I did it. This was the second time I had talked to them, but I gave names this time instead of just my pictures. I decided not to just keep the information I had on paper. I decided to pool all of my courage together and let them know what I remembered.

Along with the two agents, there was a victim advocate in the room with us as I told my story. It was amazing having her there. She interjected during the hour-long interview to check on me and respond to some of my comments to make sure that I was okay and reinforce that none of my abuse was my fault.

I gave the agents pictures to send to NCMEC that spanned from ages two to twelve in order to see if any of my images were on the internet as child sexual abuse material. The likelihood of my images being on the internet is low because of how long ago they were taken and distributed. I hope that no images will match their database, but I really need to know. I need to know if parts of me have been distributed for sick individuals to take pleasure in. I know that NCMEC will be able to tell the FBI if I am in their database, and if I'm not, they will save my pictures for any future connections that may happen.

I also brought a piece of eleven by seventeen inch paper with the history of my abuse on it to the meeting. I can't believe it all fit on one piece of paper. I'm emotional just thinking about the moment when I handed that crisp piece of paper over to one of the agents and explaining what was on it. My young life on one piece of paper. I had a list of all of the addresses I remembered and the names associated with those addresses, a list of all of the names of people I remembered, and places I didn't have exact addresses for but remember being abused in.

The agents asked how I came to find the information I was presenting, and asked me to describe a couple of the locations I remembered the most. I explained that my husband and I had gone to the neighborhood I grew up in as well as other locations I remembered outside of the neighborhood and took pictures to record the addresses. I told them that it was so emotional going to these places, that, emotionally, I could only take about an hour at a time, but I was able to get what I needed over time.

I talked about how two of the houses that I went to look at are seared into my memory on another level. One of them is an all-stone house – gray and foreboding. It has a shale roof and a dark recessed front door. I remember this house so vividly. "The basement was where the abuse took place, and there were exposed stone walls that seemed like a dungeon to my young eyes" I said. I continued with... *In fact, I think that even if I saw the basement now, it would feel like a dungeon. It was so scary as a child. I don't know how I endured the abuse I suffered without crying, without screaming, and without running away. But where would I run? I remember the cold stone below, above and on all sides of me. It smelled dank because there was a drain on the floor below the cot I was abused on. There seemed to be nowhere outside of this place. The walls closed in on me. I will never forget it no matter how much I try to.*

The second house that was calcified in my memory was my pediatrician's house and office. I described the white frame and red brick home in detail, and how it will forever be a torture chamber to me. I told them that, *the back door led to a small entryway with two seats that led to his exam room. I can only reiterate how horrifying it was. My first extensive memory of what happened in that room was the summer after I turned 4 years old. The room was bright white like the furniture. To the left of the door and backed into the corner, there was a cabinet and sink. It had three shelves above the sink area and three rows of drawers to the floor. To the right of the door, and almost behind it, was an older, scarred standing beam scale. At the beginning of every appointment, I had to step on the black platform and stand still as he stood behind me. He put his arms over my head and pressed his body to my back in order "to steady me" as he tapped the sliding black tab over to the right until the seesaw balanced in the middle. The exam table was in the middle of the room and was a tan color* with white paper pulled across it. He told me to face him, he put his hands under my armpits, and lifted me up onto the table. I hated the sound of my body moving on that paper. I still do. I lifted my arms above my head and he peeled off my shirt. I had light shorts on with an elastic band. I remember him sliding them off with my underwear after I laid down. Naked on the table he started his "exam".

On this visit, he sexually assaulted me and checked my body for any signs of infection, cuts and bruises, tears from penetration, or anything else that could require medication or follow-up care. His checklist was focused on resolving any signs that could've been observed by the outside world (that could've saved me), and any issues that could've limited my salability. I regularly left my body during these episodes. It was a technique I used as much as possible to get through it. I have no idea how long the assault lasted on that day, or most days. From beginning to end, the rituals of the appointment felt normal; I knew what to expect. After he finished the pelvic exam and his pleasure was fulfilled, he cleaned me up, zipped up and returned his clothing back to decency, and tapped me to bring me back to the present moment. I had to learn to avoid the aftermath and slide off the table. He did not normally help me down. To close out the interaction, I was allowed to pick a small toy ring or a Dum Dum sucker out of his treat drawer, and then I was returned to my mother with a progress report.

When I told my truth to the FBI agents as we went over the information together. It made me shake.

I walked them through how I took all of the addresses I found on my photography expedition, and plugged them into the Wayne County Register of Deeds. I paid by the minute and raced to find out any information I could on the property owners. I had the best luck looking at warranty deeds to find out who the previous and current owners were and the date of the exchange.

I'd recognized some of the names that popped up as abusers, so I placed them on my list of people I remembered. There were several people who also worked at my father's job, as well as other influential and affluent members of Detroit society. In addition to the names I found in Wayne County Records, I added the names of additional people that I remembered vividly. Those people included politicians, family members, and other men who worked with my father.

The agents and I went through all of the information on my paper, and I answered dozens of questions about the abusers, the locations, and my memories of other places like being taken up north to Michigan's Upper Peninsula. The exchange was so intense. I think that I knotted and unknotted the cuffs of my sweater a hundred times... maybe more.

I was told by one of the agents that she would scan in my pictures so that she could send them to NCMEC and return the originals to me. I told her that it didn't matter to me if my originals were sent in... I just wanted answers. I asked whether they would be able to update me on the progress of my case, but because it's an open investigation they couldn't make any promises of whether they'd be able to tell me anything, or how extensively they would be able to investigate. They did tell me that giving them names and addresses was very helpful which made me feel relieved.

One of the agents said she understood how difficult it must have been to gather all of the information that I did, which really made me feel seen.

So, we'll see!

I didn't leave my knowledge confined to pieces of paper.

I felt my shame lift and release its hold over me.

I feel like a warrior!

AFFIRMATIONS 3

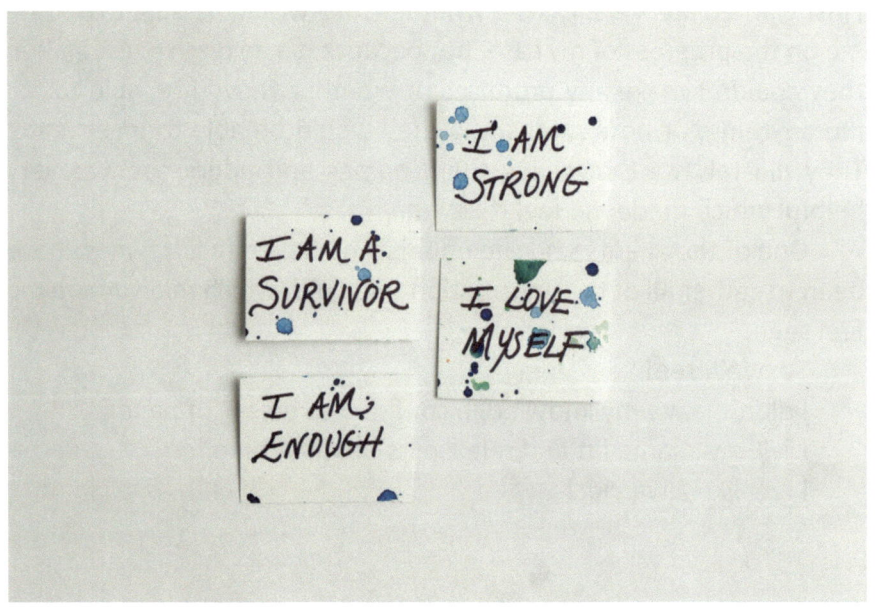

TRUCKLOADS BACK TO YOU

I have been struggling with negative thoughts about myself throughout my entire life. Sometimes I am overwhelmed by them, and sometimes I can take my inner bully's words in stride. I have found that the strongest negativity springs from a place of inner shame.

I have found myself feeling shame on so many levels when it comes to my trafficking. Shame is so insidious. It seems to bond to my cells and then it grows and grows. Finding the source of its power so that I can defeat it has been a life-long challenge. At times, shame has almost smothered me.

One of the biggest sources of shame has been how my body prepped for the rapes I endured. Before being raped, I experienced some of the same symptoms of arousal a person gets from healthy sexual activity. Whether it was from the trainer my mom put in me to make me larger to accommodate a man, another object, a digit, or someone's manhood, my body reacted and prepared for the penetration without me even thinking about it. This horrified me for decades. That coupled with my mother telling me, "You must've liked it", made me feel dirty until my therapist told me that it was just my body's natural response, like yawning when you see someone yawn. After thinking about it for months, I started to really digest what she was saying, I understood that I wasn't getting aroused because deep down inside I liked it, nor was I aroused because some shameful part of me was excited, but the symptoms of arousal were just element s of my body's reaction to a stimuli. My therapist opened my eyes to the fact that my body was actually reacting in order to protect me from more severe physical pain as a result of the abuse.

As I thought further about my biggest shame, and talked more with my therapist about it, she helped me realize that it wasn't even mine. None of it was. My body reacting naturally was not my fault or my shame. The act of raping me was not mine. The acts of mental, physical, and emotional abuse I endured don't belong to me either. I have learned that I need to return the shame and the sources of my self-hatred to the rightful owners.

I love the metaphor of taking truckloads of my shame and dropping them off at the person's door that it belongs to. I have since sent many loads of negativity from my heart and mind and permanently dropped them off. For example, I have dropped off the shame of having to have the trainer in me to my mother, I have dropped the shame of my teeth turning black to my parents for making me suffer from malnutrition, and I have dropped off the pain of anorexia and bulimia to them as well, because their actions caused these disorders. I have dropped off the shame of not knowing how to play to the many men in the pedophile ring, and I have dropped off the shame of being abused by my brother to my brother. The source of so many of my issues belongs to my parents and other abusers.

I can't tell you how much weight has been lifted from this activity, though I still have truckloads sitting in my heart waiting to be dispersed. It's work that I tend to do in waves. In between I have to take a break and grieve for my inner child and my adult self. At first it seemed like I had a void after releasing the shame, but then I found myself filling that void with my current life. I found myself creating more space for what I want to accomplish and who I want to be in the present moment.

I hope you can use this same technique to bring about more healing and growth, and I hope that as you release what isn't yours and send it off to those that were the source of your pain, that you can appreciate yourself and your strength with a new vigor. You have survived. It's your turn to live to your fullest. You don't deserve to carry the weight that belongs to another. You don't deserve it, and it's not your job to do so.

Just love yourself.

Rubble

Beige

I feel forgotten.
Hitched to depression.
Fastened to my past.
Married to the uncomfortable.

Padlocked to the lingering fumes
of a sweet potato pie,
but not tied to the crust.
The ground from which it becomes.

So, I'm groundless.
Faded.
Beige.

But is that a fact or a feeling?
A feeling or a thought?

Well...

It's a knot of thoughts and feelings,
but I admit it's not a fact.

I'm worth something.

In fact, I'm worth more than something.

Striving to live,
Working to heal,
Still hurting,
But acknowledging that my perspectives can pivot.

I'm not without worth.
And I can start living in full color.

AFFIRMATIONS 1

Trauma-Informed Care

Using trauma-informed care is an essential way for healthcare providers to connect with both victims and survivors of trauma. Victims of child sex trafficking need to feel a level of safety with a provider, a teacher, or even a friend, to be themselves in a situation that is potentially triggering. Being a person who listens to what the survivor needs, encourages a breakthrough, or welcomes any emotions that may need to be expressed, is truly a gift.

To do this, it's important to understand how trauma has the potential to present itself. A survivor of trauma can have flashbacks; an extreme startle response to sound, touch, or any other trigger; night terrors; anxiety and depression; an inability to make decisions; boundary issues; extreme and sometimes ungrounded emotions; and dissociation. The triggers that survivors respond to can be a mystery even to themselves - their minds and their bodies may just react without any control. Every person is different, and every reaction to a trigger is different, but being aware of the above is the first step in identifying trauma reactions. These reactions should generate a gentle response from a healthcare provider.

Trauma-informed care involves using non-judgmental and welcoming language and actions. Adding a personal touch to any interaction can disarm an otherwise tense situation. If you have survived a deep level of trauma, you may feel scared, closed off, and suspicious of what a provider may be asking you to do, but if the provider brings genuine warmth to the situation, that can make the interaction much easier for both of you.

It is so important for a doctor, nurse, or therapist to hold space for you, the survivor, throughout the interaction. Creating both a physically and emotionally safe and secure environment while encouraging empowerment and choice is the formula that is necessary for success. For example, you may have a hard time voicing your needs to your doctor – such as having your provider ask if it's okay to touch you and where that touch should land. You may have literally been programmed not to. Please keep trying to express your need for boundaries, and it will become easier and easier.

Your doctor or therapist should to be open and judgement free if you become activated and have an extreme startle response, or are shaking from a flashback. You deserve to have providers that remain transparent with what you would like to achieve during your appointment. Working with providers that allow you to make informed choices in difficult situations will swell empowerment within you.

Giving you the space that you need and a safe place to land, is something every provider should strive for.

If you're a provider, it may take time for a survivor to trust you and feel safe with you, but using trauma-informed care with your patient, colleague, friend, or student will go a long way towards manifesting a healthy environment of safety.

SAFETY

Safety is a loaded word when you are a survivor of abuse.

For others, it can be a soft cushion to fall into.

For survivors, it can mean

fear

insecurity

doubt...

Because I never had a moment during childhood where I wasn't a victim of child sex trafficking, I didn't know what safety felt like.

Safety can be scary for survivors because it's so different than what a victim of trauma knows. In fact, it was next to impossible for me to feel protected even when my environment was filled with cushions to fall into. I had therapists, tools in my toolbelt for healing, a safe place to live, and people in my life with whom I was forming healthy relationships with, but I still didn't feel okay. I didn't feel like I could fully be myself, or fully rest. I was always hypervigilant. The norm for me was a lack of safety. That felt right in a twisted way.

It may seem illogical and odd for a child to run away from the safe environment they were placed in after they were removed from a dangerous household, but if the new environment is so dissimilar than what they know, it can be beyond uncomfortable. It can become an environment that the child does not trust. I can't tell you how many times I ran away from safety and into the clutches of danger as an adult just because I was used to feeling helpless.

Thank goodness I have finally given myself the freedom to fully fall into my husband's arms – the most secure person I have ever known. I have let myself trust him in order for safety and peace to grow and develop within myself. It's still distressing at times to feel that security, but it's a gift that me and every other survivor deserves to receive.

LETTER TO SCHOOL, LAW ENFORCEMENT, MEDICAL, AND CHILD-SERVING PROFESSIONALS

Dear Professionals,

First, I want to thank you for all that you do in your communities. In my opinion, the people who will most likely be encountering familial sex trafficking victims and survivors are pediatricians, emergency room doctors and nurses, primary and family care doctors, OBGYNs, teachers, social workers, guidance counselors, therapists, and law enforcement professionals. I believe that those in the above professions also have the unique ability, and are in the best position, to save children and help survivors.

I want to talk to you about signs of familial child sex trafficking and ways to gain further education on this subject. I am going to present quite a few signs, and I know that some of them could end up pointing to some other type of abuse or neglect. They could also point to a disability, or they could end up indicating nothing at all. I just want to open your eyes so you'll be aware of the signs and notice them. I want you to take note so that you can act if you see a pattern that causes concern and/or warrants further action regarding a child you come in contact with, either professionally or personally.

Please also take note if you see a colleague who acts suspiciously. Unfortunately, some people become doctors, teachers, police officers, or counselors specifically so they can have access to children in order to do horrible things to them. For example, I learned about an awful situation at a local school where a counselor made the children give him hugs in exchange for help with what they came into his office for. That is a despicable grooming technique. Some parents, whether they are foster parents, adoptive parents, or birth parents, are monsters who do the similar things.

There are many clues to the abuse trafficked victims are subjected to. Here are some of the important symptoms that are *important to look out for in your students, patients, abuse cases, or any children in your care:*

- *Having a lot of sick days from school.*
- *Being frequently absent from school and activities.*
- *Taking numerous short trips.*
- *Grades going sharply up or down.*
- *Hearing different stories from the student and the parent regarding whether the student was or which illness/symptoms the student had.*
- *Going to the doctor often or not at all.*
- *Sharing that there aren't other people in the doctor's waiting room and going into the appointment alone.*
- *Seeming to suffer from malnutrition, fainting, nausea, frequent headaches, grooves in their nails, poor dental health, and/or eating disorders.*
- *Having bad hygiene.*
- *The parent(s) not showing up when the child has a medical issue at school.*
- *Bruising easily and having constant bruises that don't seem to go away; frequent injuries, cuts, burns, needle marks, or cuts that look self-inflicted; an extremely high pain threshold; being able to fix dislocations; and/or knowledge of other injury remedies.*
- *Frequent bathroom visits, sensitivity or itching in their private areas, frequent urinary tract or yeast infections, and saying they are urinating in cups or vessels at home.*
- *Having memory lapses—a lot of sincere "I don't know" responses and being dissociated or zoned out in class or during an activity.*
- *Seeming to have rehearsed responses to questions.*

- Being overly touchy with adults in a sexual way, talking about sexual things at an inappropriate age, and talking about watching others perform sexual acts.
- Being afraid of bedtime—not fear of the dark, but fear of their bed and bedtime, and not sleeping at night.
- Not being able to attend or host sleepovers, birthday parties, or other social events. Talking about spending time in tight spots like the closet, under the bed, or the trunk of their car.
- Poor ability to communicate or play with peers by first or second grade, not because they are shy but because they don't know how; avoiding social contact.
- Talking about having to wear costumes at home with frequent special parties that might be held in special rooms. The child may have names for the rooms, like "the picture room," and may say they are being photographed in the costumes; they may also be petrified to have their picture taken at school.
- Talking a lot about secrets between themselves and Dad and/or Mom
- Talking about adults coming over and staying in their room with them.
- Not being able to make choices, always deferring or refusing to make a choice, and parents not allowing the child to speak for him/herself.
- Having an exaggerated startle response to noise or touch, hypervigilance, having sensory overload episodes, and not being able to regulate emotions or behavior.
- Having non-epileptic seizures (NES) where trauma causes a seizure response. These seizures are often brought on by a trigger or flashback.
- Re-enacting abuse, physically or sexually, with classmates or friends.

- o Consistently covering up in baggy clothing or dressing provocatively.

I have suffered from every one of the above symptoms, down to having my teeth turn black and rot out of my mouth. My father used to take pliers and pull them out. Unfortunately, nobody seemed to notice. I also had no idea how to interact and play with other children. Furthermore, my pediatrician was one of my rapists, and I had no idea that true doctors don't do that to their patients, and I had permanent bruises from iron deposits where I was constantly being hit.

There are so many small children who are falling through the cracks when it comes to catching abusers and victims, and when I say there is a rampant problem in our country with children being sexually abused, I am serious. According to the Rape, Abuse & Incest National Network (RAINN), 1 in 9 girls and 1 in 20 boys under the age of eighteen are sexually abused or assaulted by an adult at some point in their childhood. Of all victims under the age of eighteen, 34% are under the age of twelve and 66% are ages twelve to seventeen.[14]

Although it is imperative to continue the "Stranger Danger" message, RAINN's website shows that children know or recognize their abusers ninety-three percent of the time. Only seven percent of reported abusers are strangers. Acquaintances constitute 59 percent of abusers while 34 percent are family members. Child victims of sexual abuse are four times more likely to have PTSD when they are adults, three times more likely to have major depressive episodes, and are four times more likely to abuse drugs than children who were not abused.15 Just like my own issues, these children's issues stem from abuse and will flower into continued problems during adulthood.

The National Human Trafficking Hotline, which is operated by the Polaris Project, compiles statistics on the trafficking tips they receive. According to the organization's 2021 Data Report, the hotline received calls regarding 16,554 trafficking victims and survivors, and 10,359 situations of human trafficking that year.16

Further research from the Polaris Project states that "From January 2020 through August 2022, 44 percent of trafficking victims were trafficked by a member of their own families and 39 percent were trafficked by an intimate partner."[17] These statistics are based on the information shared by callers to the National Human Trafficking Hotline. Again, not every caller discloses this information, and the number of children being trafficked by their family members is even higher in reality.

I am so happy there is more training now than ever before to raise awareness about abuse, and specifically human trafficking, among law enforcement, healthcare, education, and childcare professionals. In addition to the training, you may be required to attend through your job, there are many organizations that offer further training. I'll mention three of them.

The National Center for Missing and Exploited Children (NCMEC) offers in-person and online courses for law enforcement and child-serving professionals that you can take advantage of. According to their website www.missingkids.org , so far, NCMEC has trained 367,460 professionals in all fifty states and thirty-three countries, including members of 313 law enforcement agencies. The organization also has a Child Sex Trafficking Team whose resources are only available to law enforcement.[18]

The Blue Campaign is a Homeland Security campaign that raises public awareness of human trafficking. It also aims to educate and provide training for people in the retail, transportation, hospitality, law enforcement, education, and childcare industries—along with youth leaders, faith-based community leaders, and other professionals—to not only help people recognize possible indicators of human trafficking, but also to help them respond.19

The RAINN organization includes a consulting service that helps review and advise on trauma-informed programs and policies. RAINN also offers a state law generator so people can easily find the legal statutes related to child abuse and sex crimes in their state.20 Having this knowledge at your fingertips can help you know who to contact and what steps you need to take, allowing you to properly respond to any situations you may encounter.

Unfortunately, there still isn't a lot of training specifically in familial trafficking. As I mentioned in the preface to this book, there isn't a good handle on statistics for familial trafficking because it doesn't get reported to law enforcement at anywhere near the level it is happening. That's because, on average, the victims are very young, and the abuse is all they know. It is normalized. Beyond that, they are surrounded by and connected to their abusers for life.

Additionally, familial trafficking is under reported to authorities because of the daily fear that perpetrators inflict on the trafficked child. Children are literally programmed not to disclose their abuse. I am a prime example of this. It has taken forty years for me to face my abuse and bring it to law enforcement. I am not alone in this. According to an article from the National Library of Medicine, it is estimated that between 55 percent and 70 percent of survivors of child sexual abuse don't disclose their abuse until adulthood [21] I can only imagine that the statistic is similar or worse for familial trafficking survivors. You could be the person an adult survivor discloses to for the first time.

The more we are aware and trained on the nature, possible clues, and probable effects of familial trafficking, the more it can be reported to and eradicated by the authorities. It is also important to treat your patients, students, and victims in a trauma informed way. For example, ask if you can touch them before you do so. Tell them where you are going to touch next. Listen intently on what they say they need, and give them opportunities of choice to empower them. Again, you could be the first person who sees the signs of familial sex trafficking, or you could be the first person they disclose to. Make your interaction count. Let them know that you are there to help, and that you can connect them with additional help.

You may also come in contact with trafficked children and adults after the sex trafficking has physically ended. You could save someone's life by recognizing the symptoms of PTSD that come to the surface during your interaction and then offering help, referrals, or a listening ear. For example, I saw my OB-GYN constantly due to cysts, tumors, endometriosis, horribly long and painful periods, and scarring from my sexual abuse. I had many surgeries to try to remedy these issues. Every time my doctor addressed these issues, he noted that I had extensive scar tissue, especially on the left side of my uterus and pelvis. He told me he had a hard time cutting through it because it was so strong and thick; this makes sense if you know my history. A 2018 study showed that patients who were severely and chronically sexually and physically abused during childhood had a 79% increased risk of developing endometriosis.[22] If OB-GYNs have that information in mind and see evidence of extensive scar tissue, endometriosis, and the presence of severe PTSD, they may realize the patient could have been trafficked or consistently sexually abused as a child.

After I finally told my doctor about being trafficked, he said all of my symptoms made sense. He had ordered additional tests and biopsies over the years because my issues were so out of the norm, and he was trying to figure out what was going on. He also encouraged me to go to therapy and receive help for my emotional issues because I used to cry every time I saw him. But he didn't recognize how everything fit together, and I didn't disclose. I also didn't tell him about the abortion I'd had or the gut-wrenching pain I felt about not being able to get pregnant.

If my OB-GYN had known the information from the study I mentioned, being trauma- informed may have encouraged him to open a discussion that could have led me to the right kind of emotional help sooner than I did. Even though I truly and completely trusted and liked him as both a person and as a doctor, it would've let me know that it was safe to talk to him about my trafficking and my suicidal ideation sooner. No matter what, I needed the surgeries because of the diseases and physical damage, but it could've drastically changed both of our perspectives on the situation.

I had another recent trauma trigger that turned into a NES during my physical therapy appointment. There was a loud bang that seemed to shake the floor, and I immediately went into a seizure. My therapist said that she repeated my name several times and when she realized that I had gone into a seizure, she didn't panic - she just sat with me until I started to revive from it. She said all I continued to say was, "I'm sorry" over and over between my shaking and jaw tightening. The combination of me telling her in advance that I was a trafficking survivor, and the fact that she is a trauma informed professional made the situation so much more comfortable for me. Her kindness and understanding meant so much to me, and it made my recovery from the seizure more focused on the recovery instead of feeling embarrassed or misunderstood.

You may encounter an adult who shuts down because of fear when you talk to them. It could be a hint that they don't understand what you are saying. It could also mean flashbacks are creeping in, especially if you're discussing something physical. Or, they may be programmed to be agreeable and don't want to seem like they're going against what you're saying. Abuse survivors may worry that asking questions is like questioning your authority, and they may worry you will in turn be mad at them. It doesn't matter how long ago the abuse happened—with PTSD, it can feel like it's happening in the present.

You can't make people ask questions, but you can invite them into the conversation by asking if they have any. It is empowering to encourage people to speak their truth. It can make a difference during their time with you. It can also impact their future interactions with professionals and authority figures, and it can influence their daily interactions. Validation is powerful. I hope that as awareness builds regarding familial sex trafficking, it will increase public reporting and reports from the survivors themselves.

So much awareness comes from listening, observing, and creating an environment where victims feel comfortable coming forward. Believing a child who comes to you is so important. It can directly affect the outcome of a situation, both in terms of that child's freedom, and the trajectory of their healing. If a child says they are uncomfortable being around someone and they don't want to hug that person, for instance, don't assume they are being rude. They are trying to tell you something. Pull them aside and encourage them to explain why that person makes them uncomfortable or what that person does to make them uncomfortable.

When you contemplate your approach to a suspicious or concerning situation, always remember that it is not up to children to save themselves. It is not up to children to fix the child sex trafficking epidemic. It is an adult problem, and it is up to adults to fix it. It may seem like I am laying a lot at your feet in terms of things to look out for, and in terms of responsibility, but we all need to be up for the challenge in order to save lives and create real change. It takes courage to care enough to create change in an individual's life. Please know that it will also change more than the person in front of you. Helping someone affects everyone around them as well.

Courage is infectious.
It's something we want to spread.
It's something we can spread.

It is important to talk about marginalized communities whose members are being trafficked at a higher rate, especially children, people of color, people with disabilities, people with substance use disorder, the homeless population, and those who identify as LGBTQQIA+. Children, who are in the juvenile justice system or foster care are also included as especially vulnerable targets for human trafficking. When people's options are reduced and there is inequity involved, their vulnerability increases.

I also want to bring a closer magnifying glass to Indigenous trafficking. Just like there aren't accurate numbers for nationwide familial sex trafficking, we don't have accurate labor and sex trafficking numbers for those who identify as Indigenous within the United States. According to the National Congress of American Indians Policy Research Center (NCAI), a 2015 report surveyed four sites in the United States and Canada and found that 40 percent of the women involved in sex trafficking identified as American Indian, Alaska Native, or First Nations. NCAI goes on to say, "To clarify how disproportionate these rates are, it is important to note that in not one of these cities and counties do Native women represent more than 10% of the general population. And while these data are only snapshots of sex trafficking in major cities, similar trends are emerging in more remote, reservation communities."[23]

We need to join together to rally behind our most vulnerable.

The United States government's State Department puts out an annual report on human trafficking, and it is definitely a great resource to see how the U.S. and other countries are responding to this epidemic. I have read the 2021 and 2022 Trafficking in Persons Reports, and recently read the 2023 Report. When I read the 2021 report, it was the first time that I had seen a section on familial trafficking, which is encouraging. The report admits that " familial trafficking, which is unique and just beginning to be understood in the field, is difficult to identify because it takes place within family networks and victimizes children, many of whom are under 12 years of age, who may not realize they are victims...the child's inherent loyalty to and reliance on the family structure make familial trafficking difficult to identify and challenging to prosecute." It goes on to say, "Addressing familial trafficking requires an interdisciplinary approach to ensure recovery of mental and physical health, trauma-informed investigation and prosecutorial efforts, survivor-led and -centered practices and interventions, and larger societal education and awareness."[24]

Regarding the complexity of the aftermath of the abuse, the report says, "[victims] may develop educational and social delays, physical health problems, and psychological disorders such as complex post-traumatic stress disorder and attachment disorders... regardless of socioeconomic background, child survivors of familial trafficking situations often have limited avenues for resources when seeking assistance...Few resources have been developed to address the particularities of familial trafficking."[25] In other words, the government doesn't have a clear plan for dealing with familial trafficking, and neither do any of our other existing systems. We need to work together as a society to help kids who are trafficked by their families, and we need to create strategies that work.

You can help make that happen.

In the 2022 report, one of the topics was regarding survivors' stories and expertise. The report highlighted the importance of survivors, and notes that their input is a valuable asset for the movement to end human trafficking. The report states that "survivors of human trafficking play a vital role in combating this crime. Their perspective and experience should be taken into consideration to better address this crime and craft a better response to it."[26] It was so nice to read the support and acknowledgement that the government seems to have towards survivors. I hope that over time, survivor voices will be heard more and more. I know that we can make the difference needed to save more victims from the clutches of trafficking.

In further support for survivors, the 2023 report talks about the influence of a national survivor's network on the Report. The introduction "contains substantial input from the Human Trafficking

Expert Consultant Network (the Network). The purpose of the Network is to engage experts, particularly those with lived experience of human trafficking, to provide expertise and input on Department of State anti-trafficking policies, strategies, and products."[27] Secretary of State Antony Blinken states, "We can't do this work effectively without having the voices, the views, the experiences, the ideas of survivors front and center in everything that we're doing."[28]

Also, the 2023 report talks about the trafficking of boys, which is a topic that is not talked about nearly enough. It states that "boys represent the fastest growing segment of identified human trafficking victims...(and) that the UNODC's 2022 Global Report on Trafficking in Persons notes that...while women constitute about twice the percentage of identified trafficking victims as men (42 percent to 23 percent), the percentage of trafficking victims who are boys and girls is almost identical (17 percent and 18 percent, respectively)."[29] The report finds that there are less boys identifying they are being trafficked, and there is not enough support services for boys who have been trafficked. We need to do better.

It is so important for adults to listen to and validate victims of this crime. I know my situation is different from many others because both of my parents raped and sold me, but I will never forget the time I told my mom that I did not like the way my dad kissed me. I told her it was wet and sloppy, and his tongue was in my mouth. I was three years old. She got angry, told me to apologize to my dad, made me give him a hug and a kiss, and sent me outside to dig in the yard for grubs for the rest of the afternoon. I knew right then that I would never again tell anyone I was uncomfortable. That was the only time I tried.

Please embrace your responsibility to listen and believe, and do your best to do right by that child. Create a safe place where they can talk. You may be the person a child chooses to disclose to. There are resources that will help you to help them. You should relay your knowledge to the National Human Trafficking Hotline, to NCMEC's Cyber Tipline, to the many other local hotlines and organizations that work to combat human trafficking, or you can go directly to your local law enforcement agency.

I hope that writing about my experience opens eyes and hearts and helps people see what could be happening to one of their *neighbors, their students, their child's friend, or their patient. The victims can't say anything; they're children using every ounce of their will to survive. Always remember that this is an adult problem. It's not a child's problem to fix. We as adults need to be their voice. We as a community can't turn away from ugliness if we want to change this cycle of abuse. If we see something suspicious, step up and call in an anonymous tip, call 911, talk to a school administrator... do something. We need to follow our gut and then let the experts do their job.*

Progress breeds progress.
Freedom is a jewel we all deserve.
We can help save lives together.

Thank you for all that you do!

All my best,
Adira James

FREEDOM'S GEM

What is freedom?

The feeling of flight
I vicariously steal from a graceful crane?

The ease of a train
tugging its cars around the winding countryside?

Or is it the boldness
of a dancer defying gravity across a stage?

It's all of it and more.

It's walking
down the street because I want to,

Choosing
what clothing I'm going to wear,

And opening
my mouth to speak my mind gentle or loud.

Freedom catapults me
from past to present moment.

It surely isn't perfection,
But it holds the gem of possibility
In its hands.

My Voice

I have been blessed with a new relationship to my voice. Instead of it being stifled by threats from the past, I have started delivering speeches to the medical community and holding author events in order to spread awareness about familial sex trafficking and hopefully empower others to save children in need.

I can't believe that this is my reality now after being petrified for decades. Even though speaking definitely takes a toll on my emotions both during and directly after a speech or event, I love it. I love to hear the strength in my voice bouncing off the walls and back to my ears. It's refreshing after hearing so much fear for so many years. I even hope to widen the impact of my story and do speeches and trainings for law enforcement officers and academic professionals including social workers, school counselors, teachers, and other child serving professionals. I have also been blessed to be a Survivor Consultant for the National Center for Missing and Exploited Children. I hope to continue this work in the future. I can't believe how far I've come.

I have read my books out loud to myself, as well as to the public during author events. It is so healing to hear my story in a balanced way that helps others understand me. I feel heard when the audience tells me that I am helping them understand what familial sex trafficking is like. I also feel thankful when other survivors reach out to me. Because I am able to use my voice, I have had the privilege of meeting other strong individuals who have survived hell.

> With every event, speech, and sentence I write,
> I am solidifying more strength within.

In addition to shoring up my own inner strength, using my voice helps my alters see that I am on a different path. I am telling my story with the fortitude of an adult, and I am safe – nobody is going to punish me, my life is not in danger, and I am not being threatened by anyone when I tell our story. That is healing for all of us. Bit by bit, we are becoming more powerful, centered, courageous, and free.

COPING WITH TRAUMA BY HELPING OTHERS

I have found an immense sense of peace and satisfaction, increased my self-esteem, and gained a new level of strength through my service to help stop familial child sex trafficking. I have given speeches to the public, I have reached out to survivors, have spoken with survivors who have reached out to me, and I have donated to organizations like NCMEC who do such amazing work in the anti-trafficking movement.

As a survivor, I have found that helping other survivors has been very healing to me. I am a part of two survivor groups, and being able to reach out to another survivor and offer an ear, my time, or an idea that might help them, is equally healing to myself. I think that helping others is a perfect way for me to help cope with my trauma, and I think it could be an amazing way for others to cope as well.

Volunteering at organizations that help to combat human trafficking and child sex trafficking is something that anyone can do. If you are unable to donate your time though, you can also help by donating funds to organizations specializing in helping victims and survivors of sex trafficking. Whether it be through your time, or through other measures, supporting survivors, authors, speakers, and those in programs in your community is an amazing way to be a part of the movement to end human trafficking, and to help individuals in need.

Not only does helping others feel good inside, it actually benefits the brain when you give and receive help on a social level. When you give support, the activity "reduces stress-related activity in the dorsal anterior cingulate cortex, right anterior insula, and right amygdala"; it creates increased activity in the area of the brain that is part of the reward system; and "it creates greater caregiving related activity in the septal area."[30] In other words, helping others reduces stress, increases feelings of reward, and helps you care for others as you're helping them - all things that can help reduce symptoms of trauma like anxiety, depression, feelings of hopelessness and feelings of helplessness. This proves that when you help other, you are also helping yourself on a neurobiological level.

>	So, help others as you would want to be helped.
>	We can make a difference together!

EXPIRATION DATE

I've lived at least 34 years
past my expiration date.

I've outlived those that chose to
torture and use me.
Who thought they used me up
and threw me away.

But I'm here
I'm still here
Broken but here

They left me wrought with trauma
both in the flesh and in spirit.
I was discarded while being
consumed by pain.

But I'm here
I'm still here
Imperfect but here

I've died, seen the light,
and come back many times.
Rising from the depths, the swirls,
towards the light.

But I'm here
I'm still here
Emerging but here

No matter what was seized,
they cannot take away
what I've done
to surpass my expiration date.

I'm here
I'm still here
Growing roots while I'm here.

Roots and Wings

I have been devastated in the past because my childhood makes me feel like I don't have roots. It has made me feel so lost. Because I was abused from such an early age and it continued throughout my formative years, I don't have a reference for normalcy. I have no memories of a healthy childhood or a healthy relationship with myself or with my family. From a very young age, I had no reference for what healthy could even look like.

With that lack of stability as my base, I have found myself wandering in sorrow for so many reasons; feeling lost, feeling like I was robbed of what I see so many others have access to, feeling envious of the ability to reference a solid base in early life even if there was terrible trauma later on in life. In my worst moments I have felt like I have nothing to hold onto.

What I realized recently, though, is that understanding I don't have roots also means I can grow anywhere. I can make my own roots wherever I want them to grow. I can choose my family and friends that encompass the values, strengths, and balance that I want to have in my bubble.

I can flourish where I stand.
I can take flight with chosen wings.
I can develop into the human I want to be
and encourage others to do the same
regardless of where we came from.

So, let us ALL take flight!

MOUNTAIN

Hawk

ORGANIZATIONS

A21
https://www.a21.org
A21 is one of the largest organizations in the world that is solely dedicated to fighting human trafficking, and they do it on a local, domestic, and international level. They are focused on responding to trafficking that is happening now, and are trying to prevent it from happening to begin with through their Reach, Rescue, and Restore programs. A21 is focused on abolishing slavery everywhere, forever.

Childhelp National Child Abuse Hotline
1-800-4-A-CHILD (422-4453)
https://www.childhelp.org
The Childhelp National Child Abuse Hotline is available twenty-four hours a day, seven days a week. This non-profit organization has been working since the 1950s to prevent, help, intervene, and treat children who are abused, neglected, or at-risk. The organization also fosters community outreach. Its focus is on providing children with an environment of compassion and kindness in addition to meeting the physical, emotional, educational, and spiritual needs of the children they serve.

Darkness To Light
843-965-5444
800-656-4673 connects you directly with RAINN's National helpline number.
https://www.d2l.org
Darkness to Light is a leader in child sexual abuse prevention. They organization empowers adults to prevent, recognize, and react responsibly to child sexual abuse through awareness, education, and stigma reduction. It's focus is on comprehensive prevention program-

ming, advocacy for stakeholder engagement and ownership, and training to improve awareness and skills among adults.

It's A Penalty
https://itsapenalty.org/
It's a Penalty collaboratively combats human trafficking, exploitation, and abuse by using the unifying power of sports to drive local and global educational campaigns during significant sporting events. The organization also runs three core programs – *Common Protect* which advocates for legal reform in Commonwealth countries, the *Student Ambassador Programme* which empowers UK university students to combat exploitation, and *Safe to Compete*, which is co-leads with NCMEC, and educates sports coaches and parents in the USA on abuse prevention.

National Alliance on Mental Illness (NAMI)
1-800-950-NAMI
1-800-950-6264
Text "NAMI" to 741741
www.nami.org
NAMI is a grassroots organization focused on helping those affected by mental illness. The NAMI Help Line is available Monday through Friday to provide information, support, and resources for those who suffer from mental illness, their families and caregivers, the public, and health providers. It is not a crisis line, but the call-takers have the experience and training needed to guide callers to places where they can receive the help they need throughout the U.S.

National Center for Missing and Exploited Children (NCMEC)
1-800-THE-LOST
1-800-843-5678
www.CyberTipline.org
www.missingkids.org
NCMEC is a non-profit organization whose entire focus is locating and helping missing, victimized, or sexually exploited children and their

families, as well as preventing the crimes from occurring. The public can report a tip or crime to NCMEC twenty-four hours a day, seven days a week. Through NCMEC's resources and partnerships with law enforcement, mental health, and social service organizations, victims and their families can attain invaluable guidance and assistance no matter where they are on their healing journey. NCMEC also provides in-person and online classes to law enforcement and child-serving professionals.

National Child Alliance (NCA)
1-202-548-0090
https://www.nationalchildrensalliance.org/
NCA is a non-profit membership and accrediting organization that provides care through 924 Children's Advocacy Centers (CACs) and fifty State Chapters nationwide. NCA has the country's largest network of care centers supporting child abuse victims.

National Child Traumatic Stress Network
www.nctsn.org
NCTSN was created by Congress in 2000 as part of the Children's Health Act to raise the standard of care, and increase access to services for children and families who experience or witness traumatic events. NCTSN and their affiliates collaborate and work to provide clinical services, develop and disseminate new interventions and resource material, offer education and training programs, and inform public policy and awareness.

National Indigenous Women's Resource Center (NIWRC)
1-855-649-7299
https://www.niwrc.org
NIWRC is a Native-led non-profit organization dedicated to ending violence against Native women and children. It focuses on uplifting advocates' collective voices and offering culturally grounded resources, assistance, training, and policy development to strengthen tribal sovereignty.

National Suicide Prevention Lifeline
1-800-274-TALK
1-800-273-8255
www.suicidepreventionlifeline.org
This free lifeline is available twenty-four hours a day, seven days a week, for callers to receive confidential emotional help throughout the United States. It was created by the U.S. Substance Abuse and Mental Health Services Administration (SAMHSA) in collaboration with Vibrant Emotional Health in 2005. The organization continues to maintain this amazing service, along with its trusted mental health partnerships.

PACT
Protect All Children From Trafficking
1-718-935-9192
https://www.wearepact.org
PACT is a non-profit organization focused on legislative advocacy, education and partnerships to combat child sex trafficking. The organization was founded nearly thirty years ago as EPCAT-USA and has focused on the sex tourism aspect of commercial sexual exploitation of children. PACT has helped to get legislation passed, ensuring that Americans traveling abroad to buy sex with minors could be prosecuted in the US for sexually exploiting children in other countries. PACT is a member of EPCAT International, a network of organizations in over 100 countries focused on the same goal.

RAINN
Rape, Abuse & Incest National Network
1-800-656-HOPE (4673)
https://www.rainn.org
RAINN is the nation's largest anti-sexual violence organization. It created and operates the National Sexual Assault Hotline, which the public can call twenty-four hours a day, seven days a week. RAINN has programs to prevent sexual violence, help survivors, and help ensure that perpetrators are brought to justice. The organization also works

with more than 1,000 sexual assault service providers around the country and offers consulting services to assess and assist with trauma-informed programs and policies.

The Trevor Project
1-866-488-7386
www.thetrevorproject.org
The Trevor Project is the world's largest suicide prevention and crisis intervention organization for LGBTQ (lesbian, gay, bisexual, transgender, queer, and questioning) young people. They are a non-profit organization that aims to end suicide through crisis services, peer support, research, public education, and advocacy. The Trevor Project is available to help twenty-four hours a day, seven days a week.

THORN
https://www.thorn.org/
Aware that the Internet has made it too easy for abusers to share child sexual abuse material (child pornography), THORN is a non-profit organization that was created for and is dedicated to developing technologies that combat online child sexual abuse and trafficking. THORN uses its technology to protect children through three pillars: accelerating victim identification, equipping platforms, and empowering the public.

U.S. National Human Trafficking Hotline
1-888-373-7888
Text "HELP" or "INFO" to BE FREE (233733)
TTY: 711
www.humantraffickinghotline.org
This hotline is available twenty-four hours a day, seven days a week so the public can provide call-takers with tips regarding sex and labor trafficking. Victims and survivors can also receive support and be connected with services through the National Human Trafficking Resource Center (NHTRC) to help them escape their situations and stay safe. The hotline is supported by the Administration for Children

and Families (ACF) division of the U.S. Department of Health and Human Services (HHS) and is operated by the Polaris Project.
www.polarisproject.org
www.humantraffickinghotline.org/training-resources/referral-directory

United States Government Divisions, Programs, and Task Forces:

The Blue Campaign
Department of Homeland Security
1-866-347-2423
www.dhs.gov/blue-campaign
The Blue Campaign is a Homeland Security campaign to raise public awareness regarding human trafficking. It also aims to educate and provide training for those in the retail, transportation, hospitality, childcare, and law enforcement industries—along with youth leaders, faith-based community leaders, and other professionals. The goal is to help these individuals recognize the possible indicators of human trafficking, and teach them how to respond. Call the number that accompanies this listing to report suspected human trafficking to federal law enforcement.

FBI Violent Crimes Against Children/Online Predators
www.fbi.gov/investigate/violent-crime/cac
The mission of the Crimes Against Children program is to provide a rapid, proactive, and comprehensive counter to all threats of abuse and exploitation to children when those crimes fall under the authority of the FBI; identify, locate, and recover child victims; and strengthen relationships between the FBI and federal, state, local, tribal, and international law enforcement partners to identify, prioritize, investigate and deter individuals and criminal networks exploiting children.

U.S. Department of Justice (DOJ)
www.justice.gov/humantrafficking
The U.S. DOJ has many divisions and supports many organizations that focus on combating Human Trafficking. I've listed some below:

- Office of Juvenile Justice and Delinquency Prevention (OJJDP)

www.ojjdp.ojp.gov
OJJDP provides national leadership, coordination, and resources to prevent and respond to youth delinquency and victimization

- Office of Victims of Crime (OVC)

www.ovc.ojp.gov
OVC provides help to services that assist trafficking victims, and OVC aims to provide justice and promote healing for all crime victims.

- The National Council of Juvenile and Family Court Judges (NCJFCJ)

www.ncjfcj.org
NCJFCJ was developed by the National Judicial Institute on Domestic Child Sex Trafficking to further educate judicial officers on the subject.

U.S. Department of Health and Human Services (HHS)
www.hhs.gov
The mission of HHS is to enhance the health and well-being of all Americans, by providing for effective health and human services and by fostering sound, sustained advances in the sciences underlying medicine, public health, and social services.

Administration for Children and Families (ACF)
www.acf.hhs.gov
ACF is a division of HHS. They promote the economic and social well-being of families, children, individuals and communities with funding, strategic partnerships, guidance, training and technical assistance.

Office on Trafficking in Persons (OTIP)
www.acf.hhs.gov/otip
OTIP's mission is to combat human trafficking by supporting and leading systems that prevent trafficking through public awareness. OTIP also works to protect victims through identification and assistance, while also helping them re-build their lives and become self-sufficient.

Administration for Native Americans (ANA)
www.acf.hhs.gov/ana
ANA is a division of OTIP, and it is specifically focused on Native American community needs and services. As part of ANA's focus on combating both sex and labor trafficking, the administration addresses the high risk that Native American Indian, Alaska Native, Native Hawaiian, and Pacific Islander women and girls will be victims of sex trafficking. ANA has formed several initiatives, including the following:

- *SOAR Online* provides resources to help victims of trafficking and educate health professionals.

- The *Native Youth Toolkit on Combating Human Trafficking* aims to raise awareness and prevent trafficking of Native youth through safety tips, first-hand accounts, and suggested community action.

- The *National Human Trafficking Training and Technical Assistance Center (NHTTAC)* provides tools on how to respond to the specific needs of victims of trafficking and the root causes of abuse.

Internet Crimes Against Children Task Force (ICAC)
www.icactaskforce.org
ICAC helps coordinate local, state, and federal law enforcement response to exploitation of children on the Internet. Individual Task Force contacts are listed on the website by state.

U.S. Advisory Council on Human Trafficking
www.state.gov/u-s-advisory-council-on-human-trafficking/
This council was established by the Justice of Victims of Trafficking Act (JVTA) which was enacted on May 29, 2015. It provides a formal platform for human trafficking survivors to advise and make recommendations on federal anti-trafficking policies to the President's Interagency Task Force to Monitor and Combat Trafficking in Persons (PITF).

World Without Exploitation
https://www.worldwithoutexploitation.org
World Without Exploitation is dedicated to creating a world where no person is bought, sold, or exploited. It was founded in 2016 by the Coalition Against Trafficking in Women, Demand Abolition, National Organization for Women/New York State, Sanctuary for Families, Survivors for Solutions, and The Voices and Faces Project. It is a community of organizations and individuals that share a common vision and seek to leverage their skills in the fight to end human trafficking and sexual exploitation.

If you have an emergency

or see someone who is in immediate danger,

call 911 or

your local police department

NOTES

1. "Child Sex Trafficking", National Center for Missing and Exploited Children, n.d., https://www.missingkids.org/theissues/trafficking

2. Michele Rosenthal, "The Science Behind PTSD Symptoms: How Trauma Changes the Brain " Boston Clinical Trials, June 27, 2019, https://www.bostontrials.com/how-trauma-changes-the-brain/#!/

3. Elizabeth W. Twamley, MA, and Jennifer J. Bortz, PhD "Nonepileptic Seizures: Neuropsychological Mechanism", *Barrow Quarterly*, Volume 15, no. 1, 1999: 1-9, https://www.barrowneuro.org/for-physicians-researchers/education/grand-rounds-publications-media/barrow-quarterly/volume-15-no-1-1999/nonepileptic-seizures-neuropsychological-mechanisms/

4. "Child Sexual Abuse Material", National Center for Missing and Exploited Children, n.d., https://www.missingkids.org/theissues/csam

5. "Child Sexual Abuse Material", National Center for Missing and Exploited Children, n.d., https://www.missingkids.org/theissues/csam

6. The University of North Carolina at Chapel Hill, Common Reactions to Trauma, https://cls.unc.edu/wp-content/uploads/sites/3019/2018/10/Common-reactions-to-trauma.pdf

7. Wikepedia, s.v. "Hippocratic Oath" , last modified January 31, 2024 00:50,, https://en.wikipedia.org/wiki/Hippocratic_Oath

8. Jeneen Interlandi, "A Revolutionary Approach to Treating PTSD", *New York Times*, https://www.nytimes.com/2014/05/25/magazine/a-revolutionary-approach-to-treating-ptsd.html

9. "Dissociative Disorders", National Alliance on Mental Illness n.d., https://www.nami.org/About-Mental-Illness/Mental-Health-Conditions/Dissociative-Disorders (accessed 10/24/23)

10. ACE Score Calculator, "Trauma Informed Oregon, n.d., https://traumainformedoregon.org/tic-resources/ace-score-calculator/

11. David Emerson, *Trauma Sensitive Yoga in Therapy: Bringing the Body into Treatment,* David Emerson, New York: W.W. Norton, 128-129

12. Yin Yoga handout, written by Dr Shreelekha Adsule, yoga instructor

13. Stephen Parker PsyD, E-RYT 500, Swami Veda Bharati, DLitt, Manuel Fernandez, PhD

"Defining Yoga-Nidra: Traditional Accounts, Physiological Research, and Future Directions, *International Journal of Yoga Therapy*, 23 no.1, (2013,): 11, https://meridian.allenpress.com/ijyt/article/23/1/11/137857/Defining-Yoga-Nidra-Traditional-Accounts

14. "Children and Teens: Statistics", RAINN, n.d., https://www.rainn.org/statistics/children-and-teens

15. "Children and Teens: Statistics", RAINN, n.d., https://www.rainn.org/statistics/children-and-teens

16. "Human Trafficking Trends in 2020," Polaris Project, https://polarisproject.org/2020-us-national-human-trafficking-hotline-statistics/

17. "Love and Trafficking", Polaris Project, https://polarisproject.org/love-and-trafficking/?utm_medium=social&utm_source=linktree&utm_campaign=love+and+trafficking+-+polaris

18. "Training", National Center for Missing and Exploited Children, n.d., https://www.missingkids.org/education/training

19. "The Blue Campaign", U.S. Department of Homeland Security, n.d., https://www.dhs.gov/blue-campaign

20. "State Law Database" RAINN, n.d., https://apps.rainn.org/policy/

21. Lucy McGill and Rosaleen McElvaney, "Adult and Adolescent Disclosures of Child Sexual Abuse: A Comparative Analysis", *Journal of Interpersonal Violence,* 38, nos.1-2 (2022) https://www.ncbi.nlm.nih.gov/pmc/articles/PMC9723505/#:~:text=Lengths%20of%20delay%20vary%20but,and%2050%20years%20of%20age.

22. Diane Mapes, "Endometriosis Linked to Childhood Abuse", Fred Hutch Cancer Center, July 17, 2018, https://www.fredhutch.org/en/news/center-news/2018/07/endometriosis-linked-to-childhood-abuse.html

23. NCAI Policy Research Center, "Human and Sex Trafficking: Trends and Responses Across Indian Country", *Tribal Insight Brief, Spring 2016,* https://www.ncai.org/policy-research-center/research-data/prc-publications/TraffickingBrief.pdf

24. U.S. Department of State, 2021 *Trafficking in Persons Report,* June 2021: 30-31, https://www.state.gov/wp-content/uploads/2021/09/TIPR-GPA-upload-07222021.pdf

25. U.S. Department of State, 2021 *Trafficking in Persons Report,* June 2021: 30-31, https://www.state.gov/wp-content/uploads/2021/09/TIPR-GPA-upload-07222021.pdf

26. U.S. Department of State, 2022 *Trafficking in Persons Report,* July 2022: 2, https://www.state.gov/wp-content/uploads/2022/10/20221020-2022-TIP-Report.pdf

27. U.S. Department of State, *2023 Trafficking in Persons Report,* June 2023 :10,15, & 55 https://www.state.gov/wp-content/uploads/2023/09/Trafficking-in-Persons-Report-2023_Introduction-V3e.pdf

28. U.S. Department of State, *2023 Trafficking in Persons Report,* June 2023 :10,15, & 55 https://www.state.gov/wp-content/uploads/2023/09/Trafficking-in-Persons-Report-2023_Introduction-V3e.pdf

29. U.S. Department of State, *2023 Trafficking in Persons Report,* June 2023: 10,15, & 55 https://www.state.gov/wp-content/uploads/2023/09/Trafficking-in-Persons-Report-2023_Introduction-V3e.pdf

30. Psychology Today blog, *3 Specific Ways That Helping Others Benefits Your Brain* Christopher Bergland, https://www.psychologytoday.com/us/blog/the-athletes-way/201602/3-specific-ways-helping-others-benefits-your-brain (accessed 8/24/23)

ABOUT THE AUTHOR

Adira James is an indie writer who was born in Detroit, Michigan. She is the author of a memoir called *What They Couldn't Take: A Memoir of Survival From Familial Sex Trafficking*, as well as two children's books centered on child safety. James is also a survivor advocate for the National Center for Missing and Exploited Children (NCMEC). To further advocate for the innocent, she has connected with local health professionals to provide recommendations and information to combat child sex trafficking.

Now, James has a dedicated yoga practice, enjoys gardening, and uses writing and many art disciplines of art to express herself. She is happily married, lives with her husband and cat kids, and has found a new level of peace she is grateful to live in.

Made in the USA
Columbia, SC
26 March 2024

33183070R00154